Praise for SORTED:

'At a time when fewer and fewer people have learned how to
cook, yet there's more and more interest in food and exciting
flavours, the SORTED boys have managed to communicate
cooking in a new way. Their down-to-earth approach makes
an everyday necessity simple, accessible and, most of all,
pleasurable. Anyone can produce platefuls of wonderful food –
and anyone can enjoy it.'
KAREN BARNES, EDITOR OF DELICIOUS MAGAZINE

'Straightforward, wholesome, foolproof and includes cheats to
satisfy even the laziest cook.'
THE TIMES

'The SORTED team have created a cooking bible… it's humorous
and informative.'
THE SUN

'All singing, all dancing YouTube gurus who are intent on
transforming our lives.'
THE GUARDIAN

MICHAEL JOSEPH

Published by the Penguin Group
Penguin Books Ltd, 80 Strand, London WC2R 0RL, England
Penguin Group (USA) Inc., 375 Hudson Street, New York, New York 10014, USA
Penguin Group (Canada), 90 Eglinton Avenue East, Suite 700, Toronto, Ontario,
Canada M4P 2Y3 (a division of Pearson Penguin Canada Inc.)
Penguin Ireland, 25 St Stephen's Green, Dublin 2, Ireland (a division of Penguin Books Ltd)
Penguin Group (Australia), 707 Collins Street, Melbourne, Victoria 3008, Australia
(a division of Pearson Australia Group Pty Ltd)
Penguin Books India Pvt Ltd, 11 Community Centre,
Panchsheel Park, New Delhi – 110 017, India
Penguin Group (NZ), 67 Apollo Drive, Rosedale, Auckland 0632, New Zealand
(a division of Pearson New Zealand Ltd)
Penguin Books (South Africa) (Pty) Ltd, Block D, Rosebank Office Park
181 Jan Smuts Avenue, Parktown North, Gauteng, 2193, South Africa

Penguin Books Ltd, Registered Offices: 80 Strand, London WC2R 0RL, England

www.penguin.com

First published 2012
Some of the material in this book has been previously published as
Sorted: A Rookie's Guide to Crackin' Cooking and Sorted: A Recipe for Student Survival
2

Printed in Italy by Printer Trento
A CIP catalogue record for this book is available from the British Library

TRADE PAPERBACK
ISBN: 978-0-718-15892-7

MIX
Paper from
responsible sources
FSC
www.fsc.org   FSC™ C018179

www.greenpenguin.co.uk

Penguin Books is committed to a sustainable
future for our business, our readers and our
planet. This book is made from paper certified
by the Forest Stewardship Council.

BEGINNERS GET...

SORTED

BY THE SORTED CREW, WITH RECIPES BY BEN EBBRELL

MICHAEL JOSEPH
an imprint of
PENGUIN BOOKS

CONTENTS

This cookbook is crammed full of beginner's cooking that'll gear you up to create dozens of simple, cheap and tasty meals with, or for, your friends and family. Whether you're a broke and starving student, a busy professional with a tight budget and even tighter time or a parent juggling a hundred and one daily tasks, then this book will definitely get you SORTED!

The SORTED adventure began with mates around a pub table, chatting about real life, real people and real food. We don't mess around with fancy high-end dishes; instead we focus on proper grub to share with family and friends. From day one, Ben scribbled recipe ideas down on the back of beer mats for the lads to take back to uni, encouraging us to cook and eat as a group to have more fun and save some money. As word spread it was evident that more than just those around the pub table needed to try the SORTED approach to food. A cookbook supported by a bunch of online videos made perfect sense to us. So, YouTube, Facebook, Twitter and now this book became the obvious route to help us prove how much fun can be had whilst cooking with mates.

This book is supported by a fully interactive website, food hub and community at www.sortedfood.com. This is constantly updated with loads of fresh food inspiration, personal conversation with like-minded folk and all the extra bits to take you on the journey from kitchen rookie to culinary pro. Never before has getting SORTED been so easy!

SORTED recipes mostly offer a 'good bang for your buck'. Within each chapter, some recipes are, of course, cheaper than others, so we've included the following symbols as a guide:

(£) Dirt cheap

(££) On budget

(£££) Splashing out

Based on a balanced diet, the nutritional symbols below help to guide you through what's good and what's just a little bit naughty for those special occasions:

Fighting fit

Everyday grub

Occasional treat

Preparation time in minutes

(4) Serves

Follow the link to see an online clip of the recipe being prepared by the SORTED crew

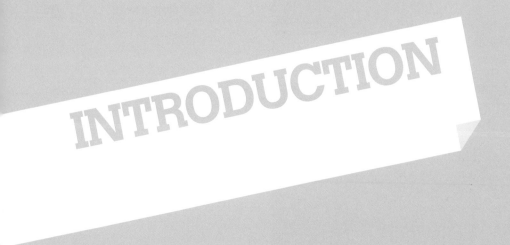

INTRODUCTION

Get Sorted.

Ben and Barry are the driving force behind the SORTED food community. Ben is a professionally trained chef with a first-class honours degree in Culinary Arts Management and eight years' experience in a multitude of kitchen environments. He now focuses on what he loves – cooking great food with his mates and helping others enjoy food as much as he does!

Barry is always looking for an excuse to party around food. As the creative director, with his passion for photography, design and style he ensures that SORTED is shared with friends around the world. Thanks to this cookbook and hours of playing around in the kitchen with Ben and the lads, he's becoming quite handy at cooking too.

Together with Jamie, Mike and the rest of the crew, Ben and Barry are here to guide you through the book and their personal help is only ever a click away online.

WE WANT PEOPLE TO BE MORE ADVENTUROUS WITH THEIR FOOD

SO ARE YOU READY TO LOSE YOUR VIRGINITY IN THE KITCHEN?

SORTED will help you build basic kitchen skills, understand essential cooking principles and produce dishes to enjoy and be proud of. Arm yourself with the musketeer knife skills to murder that onion, learn how to sizzle the ultimate steak and how to fillet a fancy fish – it's easier than you think. Then put these skills to good use through our carefully selected recipes that enable any kitchen rookie to produce fantastic grub, begin to build confidence and to get the know-how.

While actors follow the script, builders the blueprints and newsreaders are restrained by the autocue, keen rookie cooks, accomplished amateurs and professional chefs should all have the freedom to experiment a little. As your confidence grows you can begin to express yourself through food, experiment with it and have FUN at the same time. (Obviously, we're not talking about plugging carrot sticks up your nose, flicking mashed potato across the table or laughing at every curiously shaped root vegetable – although they never cease to amaze us!) By spending time in the kitchen, trying out different things and developing your own skills, it won't be long before you are a completely capable cook. At SORTED we do it our way – no frills, no nonsense, and no barriers – and we hope to inspire you to have a go too. The possibilities are endless!

To kick off let us take you through some breakfast fuel to get your motor running, wet and wild soups, mouth-watering wraps, quesadillas and sarnies. The humble lettuce leaf then strikes back with a vengeance in our salad chapter, before we up the ante and explain how to knock up the ultimate pasta or risotto and both quick and slow dishes to showcase the best meat and fish on offer! There's grub inspired from all over the world, but there are good-old steak, fish, pies, curries and stew and dumplings too. Hungry yet?

Then the devil's work hits the headlines with home-made cookies, cakes, sexy tarts and indulgent puddings galore. As if that's not enough they're all washed down with some of our shakes, punches and cocktails. We then close the book with our SORTED meal plans, proudly presented to save you even more work and designed to wow the socks off that special someone without piling on the stress and panic in the kitchen.

So once you've got your culinary mojo the only limit is your own imagination. Through our bickering, banter and brilliance we hope you'll enjoy every second spent in the kitchen, and that we can help you get . . . yes, you guessed it . . . SORTED!

EQUIPMENT

FOOD ESSENTIALS

Stuff your everyday kitchen novice will need
- Small, medium and large saucepans – best quality you can afford
- Frying pan/wok
- Colander
- Chopping boards
- Small prep knife, large knife and bread knife
- Knife sharpener
- Bowls
- Baking tray
- Dessert rings
- Roasting tray, casserole, pie dish, lasagne dish
- Wooden spoons, slotted spoon, spatula, tongs, whisk, masher
- Fish slice
- Tin opener
- Bottle opener
- Ladle
- Tin foil
- Cling film
- Weighing scales
- Cheese grater
- Sieve
- Stick blender
- Food processor
- Tupperware containers – quality, for fridge/freezer
- Skewers (wooden or metal)
- Tea towels
- Dishcloths/scourers/J cloths

Cupboard food
- Pasta – including spaghetti, penne, etc.
- Rice – white and risotto
- Noodles
- Couscous
- Salt and pepper mills
- Oil (vegetable and olive)
- Vinegar – white wine, balsamic, malt
- Flour – plain and self-raising
- Baking powder
- Dried yeast
- Dried herbs – for emergencies!
- Stock cubes
- Collection of common spices – including cumin, chilli powder, cinnamon, paprika, coriander
- Mustard
- Sauce sachets – cheese, fajita mix, hollandaise
- Tomato purée
- Pesto
- Worcestershire sauce
- Tinned chopped tomatoes
- Tinned beans – including kidney, butter, haricot
- Tinned chickpeas
- Tinned tuna/salmon/crab
- Tinned anchovies
- Tinned soups
- Tinned fruit
- Jars of mayonnaise and horseradish
- Bottle of vinaigrette
- Sugar – granulated, caster, brown, icing
- Honey
- Dried fruit and nuts

Freezer stash
- Frozen peas
- Sausages
- Sliced bread
- Minced beef
- Bacon – smoked and unsmoked
- Ice cubes
- Frozen ready-made pastry
- Frozen fruit

MAKE SURE YOU ARE WELL EQUIPPED

BREAKFASTS

Time and time again we're told that breakfast is the most important meal of the day. Eat like a king first thing in the morning and it'll propel you, your body and mind at full pace into the day ahead. Easier said than done! None of us is exactly a morning person ... in fact those who jump straight out of bed and skip their jolly way to school, university or work make us sick! So instead we have to take a different approach.

What follows are ideas for breakfasts that can be made way ahead or thrown together so easily that it doesn't matter if your eyes are still half-shut!

CHERRY AND ALMOND MUFFINS

Beat the queue and the cost of coffee shop pastries by crafting yourself some of these. This is our muffin to end all muffins, an ingenious mishmash of soft juicy cherries with nuts hidden here and there – definitely enough to keep you going until lunchtime.

Plain flour (350g)
Caster sugar (200g)
2 tsp baking powder
Pinch of salt
Pinch of cinnamon
Flaked almonds (80g)
Butter (80g)
1 large egg
Milk (300ml)
Tin of stoned cherries (400g)
Demerara sugar
Muffin cases

PREHEAT oven to 180°C.
SIEVE flour, sugar, baking powder, salt and cinnamon together in a bowl, then add most of the almonds, leaving some to sprinkle on later.
MELT the butter gently in the microwave and beat in the egg.
COMBINE wet and dry ingredients and stir to bring together.
ADD drained cherries and mix, taking care not to break them up too much.
LAY out 12 paper muffin cases on a baking tray and dollop a heaped tbsp of mix into each.
SPRINKLE with demerara sugar and a few flaked almonds and bake for 20 minutes until risen and starting to crack.
ENJOY fresh, straight from the oven or even better as a mid-morning snack the day after.

BANANA BREAD

We've never met a wimpy gorilla, and we put this ape's awesome athleticism partly down to eating the humble banana. This is because bananas are extremely nutritious; rich in potassium, riboflavin, niacin and fibre, and the rapid energy boost given by their high sugar levels means that they're a great snack. This banana bread is also a nifty way to get one of your five portions of fruit and veg a day.

Plain flour (300g)
1½ tsp baking powder
Pinch of salt
Caster sugar (50g)
Butter (50g)
2 eggs
2 ripe bananas
Handful of walnuts (50g)

PREHEAT oven to 180°C.
SIEVE flour, baking powder and salt together and stir in sugar.
MELT butter and beat the eggs.
MASH bananas and add to dry ingredients with butter and beaten eggs.
BEAT well to mix evenly.
STIR through walnuts.
SLOP mixture into a greased and lined loaf tin and bake for an hour.
TURN out of tin to cool.

OATY APPLE SHAKE

This is a guaranteed winner for all you health-conscious athletes or dedicated detoxers. A hybrid smoothie and porridge breakfast, it provides all the good stuff you need when rushing to meet a last-minute deadline or rising early for the busy day ahead.

4 cooking apples
4 tbsp brown sugar
½ tsp of cinnamon
Zest of ½ a lemon
8 tbsp porridge oats
Dollop of natural yoghurt (150g)
Just over a pint of semi-skimmed milk (600ml)

CORE peel and slice apples.
STEW in pan with sugar, cinnamon and zest for 10 minutes.
COOL the apple pulp.
TOAST oats in dry pan.
BLEND apple, oats, milk and yoghurt until desired consistency.
POUR into glass, enjoy and you're ready to take on the world.

TOP TIP
By all means cheat and buy a jar of apple sauce. Not just ideal for roast pork but perfect for this too. Simply stir the cinnamon and sugar into the pre-cooked apple sauce.

BREAKFAST 'SOOTHIE'

Your alarm rings, you hit the snooze button. The second time it goes off you know you're going to be late for lectures, or that important meeting with the boss. Again. Whether you're nursing a hangover or recovering from an all-night study session, this easy, quick, pick-me-up breakfast will do the trick.

1 banana
Handful of pecans
Tbsp honey
Pinch of cinnamon
Small cup of milk (300ml)

PEEL banana and break into quarters.
THROW into blender along with pecans and honey.
SEASON with cinnamon.
BLITZ till smooth.
ADD the milk little by little until you're happy with the consistency.
BLITZ again.
POUR into a flask and neck it while sprinting for the bus.

DID YOU KNOW?
Milk is great for hangovers as it lines the stomach and soothes any nausea you may be feeling.

MORNING AFTER ...
EGGS BENEDICT

'Who's Benedict?' we hear you ask. There are differing accounts as
to the origin of this dish, but we think his full name was Lemuel
Benedict, an American city slicker who in 1894 walked into New
York's Waldorf Hotel with a killer hangover and asked for 'buttered
toast, poached eggs, crisp bacon and a hooker of hollandaise'. The
maître d' was so impressed with the idea that he put Benedict's dish
on the menu and this simple dish was born. It's the ideal breakfast for
impressing your other half and making them think you're one hell of
a catch. Stuff it down their neck fast before they realise it's only an
idiot-proof fry-up ...

Milk (300ml)
Instant hollandaise sauce (30g)
2 large eggs
2 chunky pieces of ciabatta bread or breakfast muffin
4 hefty slices of good quality ham

BRING a pan of salted water to the boil.
HEAT the milk in a separate pan and whisk in the hollandaise powder
until smooth.
BRING to a simmer, stirring as it thickens.
STIR the salted water quickly in the pan to create a spiral effect and
CRACK an egg into the centre of the well. Allow to poach for 3–4 minutes.
REMOVE and keep warm while repeating with other egg.
TOAST pieces of ciabatta or muffin, butter them and drape the ham over
each piece.
POSITION a softly poached egg on top of the ham and spoon the
hollandaise over one side.
SERVE immediately and break into the yolk to watch it ooze.

SAUSAGE AND MUSHROOM TORTILLA

Absinthe … sambuca … tequila … Fun at the time, but come the morning after regret sets in and you want to cry 'cos your hangover hurts that much. No sane person wants to cook in this state. Stumble into the kitchen and simply warm up this fry-up alternative, which you cleverly prepared before you went out. Just whip it out of the fridge, nuke it in the microwave and invite your mates over to laugh at each other's antics from the night before. Banter, not victory, is what this meal is all about …

2 medium potatoes
1 onion
8 decent sized sausages
Shot of olive oil
Couple of handfuls of mushrooms
8 eggs
Oil for the pan

sortedfood.com/
breakfasttortilla

PREHEAT oven to 180°C.
PEEL and cut potatoes into thumb-sized chunks.
DROP into salted water and bring to boil.
SIMMER for 15 minutes till cooked.
DRAIN.
PEEL and slice onion and fry together with sausages in oil until golden.
WHACK in mushrooms and fry for a couple of minutes.
BEAT eggs in a large bowl and season with salt.
GRAB the potatoes and the stuff from the pan and stir into the egg mixture.
SHOVE the pan onto the hob, add the oil and make sure it's smoking hot before spilling in the egg mix.
LAUNCH immediately into the oven for 20–25 minutes. Once set and golden on top, take out.
ALLOW to cool in pan for 5–10 minutes.
LOOSEN around the edges and turn out.
Happy times …

WARNING!
Make sure you use an oven-proof pan – these are the ones without plastic handles.

SCRAMBLED EGGS WITH SMOKED MACKEREL

Eggs and fish? That's right. Eggs and fish. If you're not convinced by the thought of this combo, give us a chance to explain. The essential fatty oils of the mackerel combined with the protein from the eggs, all spread on a slab of carb-heavy bread, is the secret to keeping that vital organ in between your ears active. And it doesn't taste half bad either! The brain food favourite of Einstein (don't ask us to prove that), it'll give you the edge you need to keep performance levels up, whatever the task.

2 large eggs
Splash of milk
Knob of butter
Parsley
Smoked mackerel fillets (100g)
Chunky granary bread

sortedfood.com/
scrambledegg

CRACK eggs into bowl, add milk and whisk.
MELT butter in a pan over gentle heat.
CHOP parsley finely.
SKIN mackerel fillets, remove any small bones and flake into pieces.
THROW egg and milk mix and fish into pan and stir continuously.
TOAST bread till golden.
STIR eggs till the mixture thickens and mix in parsley.
ADD pinch of salt and pepper to season.
DOLLOP scrambled egg onto toast and serve with orange juice or a steaming cup of tea.

SWISS-STYLE MUESLI

OK, it's not the most appealing-looking cereal but wait until you taste our recipe! This muesli ticks all the boxes: it's quick, full of vitamins and is a long-lasting energy food that'll fill the biggest stomach. Stash it in the cupboard and it's always there when you forget to stock up on supplies. Even when your milk turns sour, just use a carton of apple juice for extra authenticity in this Swiss classic.

Porridge oats (200g)
Sultanas (120g)
Dried apricots (120g)
Chopped hazelnuts (120g)
Coconut shavings (80g)
Apple juice
Natural yoghurt
Honey or maple syrup
Cinnamon to taste

MIX the dry ingredients together and stash in an airtight container until you need it.
PLACE as much as you want into a bowl and splash over the apple juice.
DOLLOP some natural yoghurt on top.
DRIZZLE with honey or maple syrup and/or sprinkle with cinnamon.

NOTE
The dried fruit and nuts can be swapped/substituted for similar quantities of: dried apple/dried cranberries/dried mango/ banana chips/almonds/ walnuts/sunflower seeds/ pumpkin seeds.

Right … let's crack on and delve into the wonderful and whacky world of soup. Every example in this chapter and stacks more besides all materialise from one insanely simple method. Soup can be one of the quickest and easiest dishes to prepare and there are limitless varieties – there's a soup out there for everyone!

Soups are hassle-free, dirt cheap, wholesome, healthy and unbelievably tasty. What's more, you're in control! Make them to suit you, your family and friends. And for a sense of adventure, why not experiment with some refreshing chilled soups for those scorching hot summer days?

Go on, be brave!

Once you have the basic method sussed, the ingredients you choose can be manipulated again and again. This chapter explains the three key stages to creating a great soup: preparing a soup base, making a stock, then adding ingredients and flavour from our selection of soup recipes.

SOUPS

LOOKS LIKE ADAM'S A MUG RATHER THAN A BOWL PERSON . . .

SOUP BASE

The key to any good soup is the base – the starting point. For every variation that SORTED is preparing, we begin with cooking some diced onion and crushed garlic. If you're not too handy with a knife then where better to start developing your knife skills than here? Aim for a fine and controlled dice, as demonstrated. This definitely gets easier with practice. And who cares if the first few attempts aren't that neat? The whole thing is going to be blitzed up in a blender anyway! Just take your time and be careful.

Each of our soup recipes in this chapter will make at least 1 litre – enough for 4 portions. They all require the same starting point of 1 onion and 1 large or 2 small cloves of garlic.

DICING AN ONION
1 Top and tail the onion.
2 Stand it up on one end and cut down onto the board, slicing the onion in half.
3 Peel away the outer layer of skin and lay each half flat with the root end furthest from the knife.
4 Make several cuts all of the way into the onion towards its root.
5 Finish by slicing the onion in the opposite direction at 90 degrees to your first cuts, holding onto the root with your fingers well out of the way. When you're done you should have diced the onion perfectly, leaving you with just the root. You can keep the root as it's great for stocks, stews and some soups.

PREPARING GARLIC
1 Push down on the entire garlic bulb to separate the cloves.
2 Cut into the very top of a clove.
3 Squash the clove with the side of the knife and a firm hit, keeping your fist away from the blade edge. The papery casing will now easily slide off.
4 Run the knife through the peeled and slightly smashed clove, or push through a press.

FRY the diced onion in a saucepan (at least 2.5 litres) with a shot of olive oil for 2 minutes.
SWEAT the garlic off with the frying onions by turning down the heat and covering the pan with a lid for 2 minutes until the onion is translucent and soft.

THAT'S IT! Your soup base is ready.

Onion
1

2

3

4

5

Garlic
1

2

3

4

MAKING THE STOCK

Three essential stocks are vegetable, meat (chicken or beef) and fish. Although prepared slightly differently, these are fundamentally the same thing – the strained liquid from the process of simmering bones and/or meat, vegetables and seasonings. Basically, stock is the wet bit that binds our soups together!

Professional kitchens often have a stockpot simmering at all times to lob vegetable offcuts and roasted bones into. More realistically, at home you can brew up a large batch whenever it's convenient and you have the leftovers to do so, before freezing the stock down in small portions. That way there's always some knocking around when it's needed . . .

There's a classic combination of root vegetables that works with all stocks and a few things that definitely need avoiding! Onion, celery and carrot form the traditional starting point, often supported by leeks, garlic, mushrooms and tomatoes. Whole peppercorns, bay leaves and parsley stalks are also a good idea, but steer clear of potatoes and cabbage as these make the stock look like cloudy dishwater.

VEG STOCK

2 onions, halved
1 head of garlic, halved
1 stick of celery
2 carrots
Handful of leek tops
Vegetable or olive oil
Peppercorns (about 12)
3 bay leaves
Fresh parsley stalks (the bits you don't use elsewhere!)
2–3 litres of water

WASH any dirt from the vegetables you're using and chop them roughly – no need to peel!
FRY them off in a very hot saucepan with a dash of oil, stopping just before they burn.
COVER with plenty of water, add your herbs and spices and simmer for 1 hour.
STRAIN through a fine sieve, chuck the vegetables away and portion out the stock before cooling.
STORE chilled for 3–4 days or frozen for 3–4 months.

CHICKEN STOCK

HALVE the quantity of vegetables used for veg stock and add a whole chicken carcass (cooked or raw).
START by roasting the bones (if using a raw carcass) in a very hot oven for half an hour, then follow the method above.
ADD the roasted bones to your stock pan once the vegetables are coloured and continue as before.

FISH STOCK

HALVE the quantity of vegetables used for veg stock and add raw fish bones and heads.
ADD the hacked-up fish bones and heads to the browned vegetables.
BRING to the boil and simmer for only 20 minutes before straining – leave it much longer than that and the stock will go cloudy.

Or if you'd rather discreetly cheat and use a stock cube instead, go to the individual soup recipes that begin on the next page.

CHILLI SWEETCORN SOUP

1 red chilli
Thumb-sized chunk of fresh ginger, peeled
1 × soup base (see page 24)
Frozen sweetcorn, thawed (750g)
Chicken stock (1 litre)
2 spring onions

DE-SEED the chilli and dice it finely (reserving a bit to garnish later).
GRATE the ginger and add to the prepared soup base with the chilli to fry for 2 minutes.
TIP in the sweetcorn and cover with your chicken stock.
SIMMER for 10 minutes to soften the sweetcorn and release the flavours.
BLITZ in a blender, then push through a fine sieve.
SEASON with salt and pepper and garnish with finely sliced spring onions and chilli.

ROASTED TOMATO AND SMOKY BACON SOUP

16 large ripe tomatoes
6 rashers of smoked back bacon
1 × soup base (see page 24)
Veg stock (1 litre)
Fresh basil, chopped

PREHEAT the oven to 220°C.
HALVE the tomatoes, lay them on an oiled baking tray and roast for half an hour.
SLICE the bacon into strips, after removing the rind.
FRY the strips of bacon with the prepared soup base until golden. Remove a few to use as garnish later.
ADD the roasted tomatoes, cover with veg stock and simmer for about 15 minutes.
BLITZ in a blender, strain to remove the tomato skins and season with salt and pepper.
FINISH with finely shredded basil and the reserved bacon.

SPICED PARSNIP SOUP

3 or 4 parsnips (about 750g)
1 tbsp garam masala (Indian spice blend)
1 × soup base (see page 24)
Veg stock (1 litre)
Splash of double cream

PEEL and slice the parsnips – exact size isn't important so long as the pieces are all the same.
SPOON the ground spice into a pan with the soup base and fry, without a lid, for 1 minute.
LOB in the cut parsnips and cover with your veg stock.
SIMMER for 20 minutes, until the parsnips are tender.
BLITZ in a blender, season with salt and pepper and finish with cream to enrich the soup.

POTATO AND WATERCRESS SOUP

1 large potato
1 × soup base (see page 24)
Veg stock (1 litre)
Big bunch of fresh watercress

PEEL and dice the potato into 2cm cubed pieces.
ADD it to the prepared soup base and pour in the veg stock.
SIMMER for 15 minutes, until the potatoes are cooked, then submerge the washed watercress.
BRING back to the boil and cook for 1 minute.
BLITZ in a blender immediately to retain the vibrant green colour, season with salt and pepper and serve.

MINTY PEA SOUP

Bag of frozen peas (500g)
1 × soup base (see page 24)
Veg stock (1 litre)
Bunch of fresh mint
Juice of ½ a lemon

DROP the peas into a pan with the prepared soup base and cover with your veg stock.
BRING to the boil, then simmer for 3 minutes.
TEAR the fresh mint into the soup.
BLITZ in a blender, strain through a sieve and season with salt and pepper.
SQUEEZE in the lemon juice and serve.

CAULIFLOWER AND TOASTED ALMOND SOUP

¾ of a head of cauliflower
1 × soup base (see page 24)
Veg stock (1 litre)
Generous handful of almond flakes

CUT the cauliflower into florets and dice up the stalk as well. Waste nothing!
ADD to the soup base and cover with the veg stock.
SIMMER for 20 minutes, until the cauliflower is tender, especially the stalks.
TOAST the almond flakes by tossing them in a hot, dry pan until golden, then add to the soup.
BLITZ in a blender, season with salt and pepper and check for personal preference – you may want a few extra almonds as their flavour can be quite subtle.

FENNEL AND ORANGE SOUP

2 bulbs of fennel
1 × soup base (see page 24)
Veg stock (½ litre)
Milk (½ litre)
Zest of 1 orange

SAVE the fennel fronds (feathery leafy bits at the top) as a decorative garnish before you slice the vegetable.

WASH the cut fennel and add to the soup base then cover with the veg stock and milk.

SIMMER for 20 minutes to release the full flavours.

ZEST the orange and add to the cooked soup.

BLITZ in a blender, season with salt and pepper, then garnish with the fennel fronds you saved earlier.

PORTUGUESE SOUP

A simple soup, jam-packed with goodness and boasting all the creature comforts of home cooking. It's a filling bit of broth and makes a quality lunch, or even enough for dinner for you and a few mates. Go on, take on the challenge of a Portuguese meal for four!

2 big potatoes
Chorizo sausage (200g)
1 x soup base, with an extra clove of garlic (see page 24)
Big bag of kale (200g)
Pinch of smoked paprika

PEEL and roughly chop the potatoes.
CHOP the chorizo.
ADD the chorizo to the soup base and cook for a couple of minutes to release flavours.
POUR in a litre of cold water, add the potatoes, bring to the boil and simmer.
WASH and chop the kale while the potatoes cook. After 15 minutes add the kale to the potatoes.
BOIL for a further 3 minutes.
BLITZ in a blender until smooth then return to the pan. Thin down with a mug of water.
SEASON to taste with salt and a sprinkle of smoked paprika.
MOP up with crusty bread.

SQUASH AND SAGE SOUP

This is the ideal stress reliever. The therapeutic sage pauses the world around you, allowing you time to think.

1 large butternut squash
Shot of olive oil
1 × soup base (see page 24)
A few fresh sage leaves
Double cream (200ml)

PREHEAT oven to 200°C.
PEEL, de-seed and chop the squash into thumb-sized pieces.
TOSS in olive oil, a pinch of salt and roast for half an hour until squash begins to soften.
DRIZZLE in honey and heat till it bubbles.
COMBINE with the soup base in a large pan.
ADD the veg stock, squash and torn sage.
SIMMER for 20 minutes.
BLITZ to a smooth soup.
FINISH with cream and seasoning, and serve in bowl or slurp straight from a mug.

CHILLED SOUPS

Soups don't have to be steaming hot and rationed to the winter months. Here are two suggestions that follow the same basic principles as before, except they are then chilled and sipped as a refreshing light summer soup.

CHILLED CHILLI MELON SOUP

2 ripe cantaloupe melons
1 red chilli
1 × soup base (see page 24)
Veg stock (1 litre)
5 spring onions

SCOOP the seeds out of the peeled melons and dice up the juicy flesh.
DE-SEED the chilli, dice it and fry it off along with the prepared soup base.
POUR in the veg stock and add the melon and chopped spring onions.
SIMMER for just 5 minutes.
BLITZ in a blender until smooth.
CHILL well before serving with ice.

CHILLED CUCUMBER SOUP

2–3 cucumbers
1 × soup base (see page 24)
Tbsp cornflour
Chicken stock (1 litre)
3 sprigs of dill
Dollop of sour cream

PEEL and dice the cucumbers and add to the prepared soup base in a large pan.
STIR the cornflour with a dash of cold chicken stock to form a lump-free paste and add to pan with the rest of the stock.
SIMMER for 15 minutes.
BLITZ the soup in a blender and chill.
CHOP the dill as finely as possible and add to chilled soup.
WHISK in the sour cream and season to taste with salt and pepper – you could even use celery salt if you have any.

SNACKS & FILLINGS

You know the feeling – you walk into a sandwich shop and become paralysed by the choice available, so you bottle it and stick to what you know, quietly regretting another missed opportunity to step outside your comfort zone.

This chapter will help you to make a range of delicious snacks, toppings and fillings, with ideas for wraps, quesadillas, slammin' sandwiches and jacket potatoes.

TRIO OF HOUMOUS WITH CRISP PITTA DUNKERS

Remember those Greek gods and goddesses you studied in school? The ones with bodies so taut and ripped you could cut your finger on one of their six-packs? Well this is the sort of munch they ate to give them such stunning figures. To them, houmous with pitta was what beans on toast is to us Brits – low in fat and chock-full of protein and fibre. This dish can act as a quick and easy lunch, a healthy snack to be prepped before the Hollyoaks omnibus or shared as finger food at any party.

Tin of chickpeas (400g)
Juice of 1 lemon
Clove of garlic
Shot of olive oil

To vary the recipe, add the following:
Zest of a lime and 1 tbsp fresh, chopped coriander
or
Tbsp red pesto
or
Tsp ground cumin and ½ tsp chilli powder

DRAIN and rinse chickpeas and empty into food processor.
ADD lemon juice.
CRUSH peeled clove of garlic and add to the mix.
BLITZ with olive oil until a smooth paste.
SEASON with salt and pepper and divide into 3 bowls.
BEAT the ingredients for each variation into the separate bowls.
CRISP a few pitta breads in the toaster and cut into dunking strips.
ENJOY as a casual lunch or for a healthier option to pre-dinner nibbles.

HOMEMADE ONION RINGS

All the best ideas start in the pub – everyone knows this ... But why? Is it the relaxed atmosphere? The intoxicating liquids? Or is it the comfort of seeing a few familiar friendly faces?

We think there's something else ... the food. Pub food is what makes Britain great. It's simple, it's tasty and you can be guaranteed to find the same dishes in pubs up and down the country. This makes it feel like home, and when you're at home you're relaxed. It opens your mind to new opportunities and daft ideas ... like writing your own cookbook with a group of mates!

Anyway, this brings us on nicely to onion rings – the ultimate pub snack. Thin circles of white onion, smothered in a gorgeous beer batter and then fried until golden and crispy. Perfect for soaking up the copious amounts of alcohol you consume whilst dreaming up your plans of world domination.

Vegetable oil for deep-frying
2 large onions
Beer (175ml)
Plain flour (150g)

HEAT up the oil in a saucepan, taking care to only half-fill. (Never leave this unattended and if the oil begins to shimmer or smoke, remove from the heat immediately.)
PEEL the onions and slice across to create chunky slices. Separate into individual onion rings.
WHISK the beer into the flour until lump-free, adding a pinch of salt.
DUST the onion rings in a little extra flour and dunk into the batter.
LOWER carefully into the hot oil and fry for 3–4 minutes, until golden.
SCOOP the rings out of the oil with tongs or a slotted spoon, drain them on kitchen paper to remove excess oil and sprinkle with a little salt.

IT'S NACHO TIME

As part of our quest to spread the SORTED love we trekked up and down the country and cooked dishes with and for the people we met, inspired by their social environments. Loughborough University was always a popular destination, the academic home for one of the crew and a sort of theme park of the university world. This crazy campus is a playground that oozes fun by the bucketload. So keep your energy levels annoyingly high and indulge in some quick party food. An exciting nacho platter accompanied by a truckload of dunkable dips all loaded with melted cheese. What better way to stock up on your calorie count whilst lining your stomach for the mayhem to follow?

The Basics
Big bag of tortilla chips
Wedge of hard cheese (Monterey Jack or Cheddar)
Jalapeño chillies
Sour cream

Tomato salsa
1 red onion
1 red chilli
Handful of ripe tomatoes
Clove of garlic
Sprinkle of fresh coriander
Pinch of sugar
Juice of ½ a lime

Guacamole
3 ripe avocados
Juice of 1 lemon
Clove of garlic, peeled and crushed
2 tomatoes, diced
Pinch of cayenne pepper

PEEL and finely dice the onion, chilli, tomatoes, garlic and coriander.
MIX together with salt, pepper, sugar and lime juice.
HALVE the avocados, remove stones, scoop out flesh and mash, then combine with the other guacamole ingredients.
SCATTER a large plate with tortilla chips.
GRATE over a generous helping of cheese and fling on some chopped jalapeños.
HEAT in microwave or under a low heat grill to melt the cheese.
DOLLOP with sour cream, salsa and guacamole and let everyone dive in and graze.

BUILD YOUR OWN PIZZA

Instead of forking out for a Domino's and caking each slice in the free sauce why not save some dollar and make your own? This pizza dish embodies the SORTED ideology of social cooking more than most – everybody gets involved. Whip up some bases, throw together an array of toppings and scatter on the table for your mates to construct their own, then launch into the oven. A sure-fire way to stop giving your hard-earned cash to the local pizza joint and bring you and your friends closer together as you catch up over some DIY food.

Dough
1½ tsp dried yeast (7g)
½ tsp sugar
Lukewarm water (approx 250ml)
Plain flour (500g)
4 tbsp olive oil
Tsp salt

Tomato base
1 onion
2 cloves of garlic
Shot of olive oil
Tin of chopped tomatoes (400g)
Tbsp mixed dried herbs
Toppings of choice

sortedfood.com/
pizza

MIX the yeast, sugar and roughly a quarter of the warm water in a bowl and leave for 10 minutes.

SIEVE flour into another bowl, adding oil and salt.

POUR in the yeast mixture and enough of the leftover warm water to bind the ingredients.

KNEAD until you have a smooth dough.

COVER the dough with a clean cloth and leave the yeast to do its magic for about an hour.

PEEL and dice the onion and garlic, then sweat in a pan with the oil until translucent.

DUMP in the tomatoes and herbs and simmer for half an hour to reduce consistency.

PREHEAT the oven to 220°C.

BREAK OFF a quarter of the dough, roll out to form a thin base and place on an oiled baking tray.

BAKE in the oven for 5 minutes. At this stage you can keep the bases in the fridge or even freezer until you require them. Make a stash – a really handy supper.

SPREAD the tomato sauce to the edges of the base, sprinkle with grated cheese and your choice of topping.

BAKE for 10–15 minutes in the oven until golden and crisp.

THE ULTIMATE JACKET

Nothing beats a hot, fluffy jacket potato with crispy skin, served with a generous dollop of chilli con carne and grated cheese on Bonfire Night. And that's what we've got here – but remember, remember, it's not just limited to the fifth of November. Nor just chilli. Here's how to make the best comfort food going!

A WINNING RESULT

1 The best potatoes to use are the white, floury, non-waxy ones – like Maris Piper or King Edward.
2 Shape and size really do matter! Go for a round potato rather than an elongated flat one and aim for something around 400g in weight.
3 Preheat the oven to 190°C. Scrub the potatoes clean, then prick them all over with a fork to stop the skins bursting as they cook.
4 Season some olive oil and use it to rub over the pricked skins.
5 Bung the potatoes onto the middle shelf of the hot oven for 1½ – 2 hours, turning over half way through.

CUTTING CORNERS

Of course, if you can't handle the hunger pains long enough to bake a potato the traditional way, then preheat the oven to 220°C while you run through points 1, 2 and 3. Then nuke the spud in the microwave on full power for 8–10 minutes. Now rub in seasoned oil and crisp up in the preheated oven for at least 20 minutes, until you just can't survive the wait any longer!

FANCY A TOPPING OR A FILLING?

The same thing? Oh no. We reckon that if you scoop out the cooked flesh, mix it with your ingredients and refill the skins then it's a filling. A dollop of something slopped over the cut potato would be a topping. Simple! The following pages include some popular options.

JACKET FILLERS

CHILLI CON CARNE

1 large onion
2 cloves of garlic
1 red chilli
Olive oil
1 green pepper
Tsp chilli powder
Tsp ground cinnamon
Tsp ground cumin
Beef mince (500g)
Large glass of red wine
Tin of chopped tomatoes (400g)
Squeeze of tomato purée
Tin of kidney beans (400g)
4 × ultimate jackets (see page 55)
Grated cheese, sour cream or guacamole to serve

PEEL and dice the onion and garlic and chop up the chilli, keeping the seeds in.

FRY them all in a large deep pan with a shot of olive oil.

DE-SEED and chop the green pepper and add this to the pan.

SPOON in the spices and mix, then add the minced beef.

FRY for 3–4 minutes before you slosh in the red wine.

TIP in the tomatoes, a cup of water and a squeeze of tomato purée.

BUBBLE the mixture for at least an hour before adding the drained and rinsed kidney beans.

SIMMER for a further hour, then season with salt and pepper and serve over ultimate jackets, topped with grated cheese, sour cream or guacamole.

STORE any leftovers in the fridge – it tastes even better the next day!

CREAMY BRIE MUSHROOM FILLING

½ an onion
Olive oil
Clove of garlic
Large handful of button mushrooms
Double cream (about 50ml)
Couple of fresh chives
Wedge of brie cheese
1 × ultimate jacket (see page 55)

PEEL and dice the onion as finely as you can and fry in a pan with a dash of oil for 2 minutes.

PEEL and crush the garlic, add to the pan and fry for another minute.

HALVE the mushrooms and fry until soft.

POUR in the cream, then add some black pepper and finely sliced chives.

BREAK up the brie into the pan and heat it until it all melts.

SCOOP the cooked flesh from the halved ultimate jacket while still hot and place in a bowl.

ADD the brie-mushroom mixture, stir through and then re-fill the potato skins.

RETURN to the oven to colour the top and serve immediately with a crisp salad.

PRAWN AND SPRING ONION FILLING

Handful of frozen cooked prawns
Couple of spring onions
Few sprigs of fresh parsley
1 × ultimate jacket (see page 55)
Tbsp mayonnaise
Sprinkle of paprika
Butter

THAW the prawns and squeeze out any excess liquid.

CHOP the spring onions and parsley as finely as possible.

SCOOP the cooked flesh (that's the potato bit in the potato) from the halved ultimate jacket while it's still hot and place in a bowl. Keep the skins for later.

MIX the prawns, mayo, onions, parsley and paprika into the potato flesh.

SEASON with salt and pepper then re-fill the skins.

DOT the top of the potato with a couple of tiny knobs of butter, then return to the hot oven for 10 minutes to go golden brown.

SERVE immediately with a crisp salad.

TUNA SORRENTO

Tin of tuna (185g)
Tin of red kidney beans (210g)
Bunch of spring onions
Dollop of mayonnaise
Shot of olive oil
1 x ultimate jacket (see page 55)

(£) (◡) (5) (2)

DRAIN tuna and drain and rinse kidney beans and put in a bowl.
CHOP the spring onions and add to the tuna-bean mix along with the mayonnaise.
SEASON with salt (be careful – if the tuna was in brine it may not need salt) and pepper and mix well.
SLASH open the potato and load on the topping.

TOP TIP
Don't forget that, as with most of these fillings, this would also work well in a sandwich or wrap.

WRAPS

If mums made packed lunches this good, school dinner ladies would be out of a job. So scrimp on your pennies and take our advice with this ultimate packed-lunch wrap. Make this first thing in the morning and wrap up for later. Be warned though, they're so good you'll need sheer willpower to stop yourself scoffing 'em there and then.
Each of the fillings below is enough to fill 1 x 25cm tortilla wrap.

CALIFORNIAN RANCH

With an irresistible mix of avocado, ripe tomato and cold meats spread on a bed of cream cheese and wrapped in a soft tortilla, these Californian ranch wraps will have you dribbling for more.

1 ripe avocado
2 ripe tomatoes
Small tub of garlic and herb cream cheese
Pack of pre-cooked sliced turkey or chicken

SPREAD the cream cheese over one side of each tortilla, going right to the edges.
HALVE the avocado, remove stone and scoop out flesh.
SLICE lengthways.
DRAPE the cooked turkey or chicken in a line across the wrap and top with the avocado pieces.
SLICE the tomatoes and lay them on top of the line of other ingredients.
ROLL up tightly and pin in place with cocktail stick (not essential).
PACKAGE up in tin foil and head on your way knowing lunch is one less thing to worry about.

HOISIN CRAB WRAPS

For an oriental twist, try this crab drizzled in hoisin sauce – your mates will think you're a chef par excellence.

Tin of crab meat (185g)
2 tbsp mayonnaise
1 tbsp hoisin sauce
¼ a cucumber
2 spring onions

SQUEEZE as much brine from the drained crab meat as possible.
BEAT together the mayo and hoisin sauce.
SPREAD the hoisin/mayo over the wraps, smearing it to the edges.
SPOON the crab into a line across the wrap.
SLICE the cucumber and spring onion into strips and arrange on top of the crab.
ROLL the wrap up tightly and pin in place with a cocktail stick (not essential).
PACKAGE up in tin foil ready for your day.

CHICKEN CAESAR

Handful of crisp lettuce leaves – little gem or cos varieties are perfect
1 cooked chicken breast, sliced
4 anchovies
2 tbsp Caesar dressing
Sprinkling of Parmesan shavings

TEAR the lettuce leaves into pieces.
MIX all the ingredients together in a bowl.
PILE the filling into your tortilla wraps and enjoy.

DUCK AND PLUM SAUCE

4 spring onions
½ a cucumber
Shredded duck meat, about half a cooked breast
4 tsp plum sauce or hoisin sauce

SLICE the spring onions across finely and cut the cucumber into
matchstick-sized pieces.
ARRANGE on the wrap.
MIX together the duck and the plum sauce and spoon onto the wrap
before folding.

CHILLI CRAB

Tin of white crab meat (170g)
1 lime
½ a red chilli
Sprig of fresh coriander
Dollop of mayonnaise to bind
Crisp lettuce
Couple of slices of tomato

DRAIN the crab meat and place in a bowl.
ZEST the lime into the bowl.
DE-SEED and dice the chilli and chop the coriander.
COMBINE with the mayo and crab meat in the bowl, season well with
salt and pepper, then make up your wraps with lettuce and tomato.

QUESADILLAS

Little cheesy thing. Three words which, when muttered from a girl's mouth, will crush any guy's ego. However, it is also the literal Spanish translation for a quesadilla (pronounced kay-sar-dee-ah) – a panini-style Tex-Mex dish. Makes great party finger food, hot or cold. Just don't let it slip that the dish's name really means 'shrivelled Wotsit' in Spanish.

This recipe has become a SORTED staple. It makes regular appearances during our live food demonstrations, and every time we share the recipe people are stunned at how quick, simple, versatile and tasty they are. They usually contain a mixture of chicken, cheese and chilli, but we think that anything that works on a pizza will be great in a quesadilla. Just pick your ideal pizza topping from the takeaway menu and rustle up your own version for a fraction of the price. Don't get left behind … try one yourself!

Here's the basic method, followed by our favourite fillings. Each makes enough for one quesadilla.

LAY out a tortilla and sprinkle with a handful of whichever cheese is listed for your filling.
SCATTER your additional chosen filling over and finish with more cheese.
WHACK another tortilla on top and fry in a medium pan with a spot of oil, turning once, until crisp.
QUARTER into portions and serve with your preferred dip.

SPICY CHICKEN

½ a chicken breast
Cajun spice mix
Shot of olive oil
½ a red onion, peeled
½ a red pepper
½ a red chilli
Handful of coriander

sortedfood.com/
chickenquesadilla

SLICE chicken as thinly as possible.
SPICE chicken with Cajun spice mix, rubbing into the meat.
SIZZLE marinated chicken in a hot, oiled pan to cook through.
CUT onion, pepper and chilli into thin strips.
MIX everything together and sprinkle with coriander.

SWEET POTATO AND BLUE CHEESE

Small sweet potato
Chunk of blue cheese
½ a red onion

PEEL the sweet potato and dice into 1cm pieces.
PLACE in a pan of salted cold water.
BRING to the boil and simmer for about 8 minutes, until the potato is cooked through.
DRAIN the potato and leave to cool.
COMBINE with crumbled blue cheese and finely sliced onions.

RED ONION MARMALADE AND GOAT'S CHEESE

3 red onions
Shot of oil
Brown sugar (50g)
Balsamic vinegar (50ml)
Glass of red wine (150ml)
Goat's cheese (100g)
Fresh basil

PEEL and slice the red onions, then fry in a pan with the hot oil for 5 minutes, until softened.
SPRINKLE in the brown sugar, then add the vinegar and wine.
SIMMER for 15 minutes, until the onions have a syrupy consistency, then cool.
CRUMBLE the goat's cheese into a bowl.
PICK a handful of fresh basil leaves and combine all ingredients.

HAM, MUSHROOM AND TARRAGON

2 or 3 field mushrooms
Butter
Few slices of cooked ham
Sprig of fresh tarragon

SLICE the mushrooms and fry in a hot pan with a knob of butter so they go a golden colour.
SEASON well with salt and pepper.
CUT up the ham.
PLUCK the leaves from the tarragon stalks, chop finely and mix together.

SLAMMIN' SANDWICHES

A packed lunch doesn't have to be a sandwich, but if it is then make sure it's homemade! Of course, we don't always have time to bake our own bread – but try to at least find time to make your own sarnies, as the ones you buy from shops can be expensive, high in salt and brimming with saturated fats. And while you're at it, you can make it just the way you like it. For a little inspiration, here are some of our favourite sandwich fillings.

MANGO CHICKEN

1 cooked chicken breast
Dollop of mayonnaise
Tbsp mango chutney
Handful of fresh coriander

DICE the chicken into pieces and dump into a bowl.
SPOON in equal quantities of mayo and chutney, season with salt and pepper and mix together.
TEAR up the coriander leaves and mix these through too.

AVOCADO AND BACON

3 rashers of smoked bacon
1 ripe avocado
¼ of a red onion
Tsp mayonnaise

GRILL the bacon on a wire rack until golden and crispy.
HALVE the avocado, remove the stone and scoop out the flesh.
SLICE the avocado and peel and slice the onion fairly finely and mix in a bowl with the mayo.
SPOON the filling onto the bacon, wedged between two thick slices of brown bread.

SPICED TOMATO CHUTNEY

If you fancy going the extra mile and making your own chutney, here's how ...

Clove of garlic
1 red onion
1 red eating apple
Ripe tomatoes (500g)
Small handful of sultanas
Tsp grated fresh ginger
Tsp mustard seeds
Pinch of ground cloves
Brown sugar (100g)
Malt vinegar (250ml)

PEEL and grate the garlic.
PEEL and dice the red onion and apple.
CHOP up the tomatoes.
PUT all the fruit, vegetables and dry ingredients into a deep pan with half the vinegar.
BRING to a simmer and cook for 45 minutes.
ADD the remaining vinegar and cook for a further 30 minutes, until the mixture is a syrupy consistency.
POUR into clean jam jars and cool.
STORE in the fridge for up to 3 months, using it alongside cooked meats and cheese in sandwiches.

TOP TOASTIES

A brilliant toastie machine can help you to create a shedload of warm, comforting snacks that hold just about anything you like.
So quick to use and requiring nothing more than a quick wipe-down afterwards, the toastie machine is a little godsend.

Simply butter two slices of bread, lay one slice butter-side down on the preheated cast-iron plate and arrange your filling on top. Complete with the other slice of bread (butter-side up) then carefully close the lid, set the timer for 4 minutes . . . and it's job done!

HAM AND EGG

Sounds risky but this works a treat. Once you've cracked it, you'll be hooked!

1 egg
Couple of slices of cooked ham

PUSH the base layer of bread down into the grooves of the toastie machine.
CRACK the egg into this well, moving the yolk to one side and the majority of the white to the other.
LAY the ham slices over the egg, taking care not to break the yolk, and cover with the second slice of bread.
COOK for 4–5 minutes to create a perfectly baked egg held within the bread. Best served with ketchup.

BANANA AND PEANUT BUTTER

You're not restricted to savoury toasties. Bread works well in numerous puddings and this is no exception. Try this sweet little number and you won't look back.

1 small banana
Tbsp crunchy peanut butter

SLICE the banana quite thinly and arrange on the bread.
SPREAD the peanut butter across the toastie and top with the bread lid.
COOK as normal and enjoy for dessert with a scoop of vanilla ice cream.

CHEESE AND MUSHROOM

The oils released from the cheese will cook the mushrooms perfectly in the 4 minutes.

2 mushrooms
Cheddar cheese (50g)
2 spring onions

WASH the mushrooms and slice them as finely as possible.
SLICE the cheese so you have enough to cover the base of the toastie.
CHOP the spring onions.
LAY the cheese on the bread, top with mushrooms and then finish with chopped onion.

SALADS

You don't need to be a ravenous rabbit to appreciate a good salad.

We are delighted to present here some of the SORTED Crew's favourite salad ideas. These will hold their own on the barbecue spread, claiming their rightful place alongside the ever-so-slightly-overdone sausage, chicken skewer and monster burger. Or they can be the subject of true envy at lunch as you nonchalantly whip out a tub of your own salad creation to trump the supermarket alternatives of your friends.

Once you've got the foundations of the salad, whether that's pasta, potato, couscous or beans, the rest is up to you. Dress it in vinaigrette, flavoured mayonnaise or pesto, and bulk it out with anything vibrant and fresh. We're aiming for colour, flavour and texture here to ensure these salads are the business.

Any rabbit that gets hold of one of these salads will be as lucky as . . . well . . . his own back foot!

STUNNING SALADS
FOR THE SCORCHING
SUMMER SUN

SALAD FOUNDATIONS

COOKING DRIED PASTA

1 For a main-course portion allow 100g of pasta per person, or about 50g per person for a salad. Aim for about a litre of salted water in the pan per 100g of pasta.

2 Only add the pasta once the water is boiling rapidly and then stir for 30 seconds to make sure the pasta doesn't stick to itself or to the pan. A rapid boil is important throughout. Set the timer for a minute less than it states on the packet, then test the pasta by trying a piece.

3 Drain into a colander and run under cold water to cool immediately if using for a salad, or immediately toss into your chosen sauce if serving hot.

BOILING POTATOES

1 Make sure all the potatoes are scrubbed or peeled and cut into the same-sized pieces to allow even cooking.

2 Place in a pan and cover with cold water plus a pinch of salt. Bring to the boil and gently simmer for 15–20 minutes for regular potatoes or 12–15 minutes for small new potatoes. They're ready when a sharp knife glides into the centre without resistance but the potato still holds its shape.

3 Drain in a colander and stop the cooking process quickly under cold running water.

COOKING COUSCOUS

1 Allow 50g of couscous per serving.

2 Work out the volume by tipping your couscous into a measuring jug, then pour into a bowl and cover with an equal volume of boiling water or stock (see page 23). Stir to ensure that all the grains are submerged then cover the bowl with a lid, plate or cling film.

3 Leave to stand for 3–4 minutes. Fluff up the couscous with a fork and add the required flavourings.

Pasta

2

3

Potatoes
1

2

3

Couscous
1

2

3

PASTA SALADS

OLIVE, CAPER, ANCHOVY AND BASIL

Bowl of cooked and cooled pasta shapes (100g)
Drizzle of extra virgin olive oil
2 tbsp capers
Handful of stoned black olives
Anchovy fillets (about 6)
Bunch of fresh basil
Chunk of Parmesan

LUBRICATE the pasta with the oil in a large bowl, to stop all the pieces
bunching together.
DRAIN the capers and the olives.
CHOP up the anchovy fillets and halve the olives.
TEAR the basil and stir the leaves through the pasta with the capers,
olives and anchovies.
GRATE over the parmesan and combine everything.
SEASON with pepper, avoiding salt because of the anchovies, and enjoy.

Allowing the flavours to infuse for an hour or so at room temperature
improves this salad no end.

HAM, BROAD BEAN, CHIVE AND SOUR CREAM

Bowl of frozen broad beans
Cooked ham (50g)
Bunch of fresh chives
Bowl of cooked and cooled pasta shapes
Dollop of sour cream

THAW the beans at room temperature.
SLICE the ham into slivers and snip the chives, then stir them into
the pasta.
POP the beans out of their tough skins, leaving just the succulent,
vibrant beans.
ADD to the pasta with enough sour cream to just bind.
SEASON well with salt and pepper.

POTATO SALADS

CHERRY TOMATO AND ROCKET

New potatoes, skin on (1kg)
Vinaigrette (French dressing)
Big handful of fresh rocket
Cherry tomatoes (about 250g)
1 red onion

BOIL the potatoes and drain when cooked.
SHAKE the dressing well and drizzle over the warm potatoes.
They will absorb the flavour as they cool.
RIP up the rocket and halve the tomatoes.
PEEL and slice the red onion as finely as possible.
MIX all the ingredients together when the potatoes are cold,
then season with salt and pepper and serve.

BEETROOT, HORSERADISH AND WATERCRESS

New potatoes, skin on (1kg)
Cooked beetroot (not in vinegar) (250g)
Bunch of watercress
2 dollops of mayonnaise
Tbsp hot horseradish sauce

BOIL the potatoes until cooked.
CHILL the potatoes and cut them into bite-sized pieces.
DICE the beetroot and stir into the potato.
WASH and roughly chop the watercress, stalks included, then add to
the salad.
COMBINE the mayo with the horseradish. The ratios depend on
personal preference but remember the dressing will mellow down when
added to the potato. Twice as much mayo as horseradish is a safe start.
SEASON the salad with salt and pepper and bind it all together with
the mayo and horseradish mixture.
TASTE and adjust horseradish and salt levels before serving.

COUSCOUS SALADS

SPINACH, PINE NUT AND LEMON

Couple of handfuls of fresh spinach
Couscous (100g)
Equal volume veg stock
Handful of pine nuts
1 lemon
Bunch of fresh parsley

COOK the couscous in the veg stock (see page 86 for method).
WASH the spinach to free it from grit and add it to the couscous as it
is cooking so that the spinach begins to wilt.
TOAST the pine nuts in a dry pan to give them a golden colour.
SQUEEZE the lemon into the couscous bowl with a generous amount
of black pepper.
CHOP the parsley finely and stir through the salad with the toasted
pine nuts.

CHORIZO, FETA AND SPRING ONION

Couscous (100g)
Equal volume chicken stock
Chunk of chorizo
Slab of feta cheese
A few spring onions

COOK the couscous in the chicken stock (see page 86 for method).
REMOVE the papery skin of the chorizo and hack the sausage into
small bite-sized chunks.
FRY them off in a dry pan for a couple of minutes to release loads of
tasty, spicy oils.
STIR the sausage and all of its oil into the cooked and fluffy couscous
to infuse flavour and impart colour.
CRUMBLE the feta and finely slice the spring onions.
MIX everything together, loosening with a little extra oil if necessary,
and season well with salt and pepper.

VEGETABLE PESTO COUSCOUS

You're at the gym for the first time in donkey's years and you go for that pre-session weigh in. Alarm bells ring and you panic as you try to mentally organise a healthy eating plan. Well, for a start, look no further than this veggie pesto couscous – an ideal way to begin a detox. Light, full of flavour and, best of all, low in calories, it's tasty enough to fill you up without having to fight your conscience. Effortless healthy eating …

1 red pepper
1 yellow pepper
1 medium aubergine
1 medium courgette
1 red onion
3 cloves of garlic
2 shots of olive oil
Couscous (200g)
Equal volume veg stock
2 tbsp of green pesto

PREHEAT oven to 220°C.
HACK up all the vegetables into irregular-shaped mouth-sized pieces and throw into a deep baking tray.
TOSS in olive oil.
PEEL and crush the garlic over the veg.
ROAST in oven for 15 minutes.
PREPARE the couscous (see page 86 for method).
TIP in the roasted vegetables and pesto.
STIR, season and allow to cool completely.
STORE in tupperware for the perfect picnic in the park, travel snack or post-gym boost.

OTHER SALADS

THREE BEAN SALAD

Tin of kidney beans (400g)
Tin of butter beans (400g)
Handful of fresh French beans
Bunch of spring onions
Clove of garlic
Drizzle of vinaigrette

DRAIN the tinned beans in a colander and rinse under cold
running water.

FILL a pan with salted water and bring to the boil.

SNIP the tops and tails off the French beans, finely slice the spring
onions and peel and grate the garlic.

COOK the French beans in the rapidly boiling water for 2–3 minutes,
then drain them under cold running water to cool immediately. They
should still have a 'bite' to them.

CUT the cooled beans into pieces similar in size to the kidney beans and
combine all the ingredients in a bowl.

SEASON well with salt and pepper and serve.

APPLE AND CELERIAC COLESLAW

Medium celeriac
3 red eating apples
1 red onion
2 sprigs of fresh dill
2 tbsp mayonnaise
Dollop of wholegrain mustard
1 lemon

CUT away the tough outer layer from the celeriac and coarsely grate the vegetable.
WASH and core the apples, peel the onion and grate both.
CHOP the fresh dill finely, then combine all the prepared ingredients in a bowl with the mayo and enough mustard for personal taste.
SEASON with a squeeze of lemon juice and plenty of salt and pepper.

ASIAN BEAN SPROUT SALAD

½ a cucumber
Handful of radishes
Thumb-sized knob of fresh ginger
Tbsp sesame oil
2 tbsp caster sugar
2 tbsp soy sauce
1 fresh red chilli
Tbsp lime juice
Plenty of fresh bean sprouts

WASH the cucumber, halve it lengthways and scoop out the seeds and centre flesh (chuck these out as they will make the salad soggy).
SLICE the radishes finely and cut the cucumber into matchsticks to resemble the bean sprouts.
PEEL and grate the ginger into a large bowl and mix in the oil, sugar and soy sauce.
REMOVE the seeds from the chilli and chop it up as finely as possible. Add to the dressing.
SQUEEZE in the lime juice, stir, then pour over all the prepared ingredients and bean sprouts and toss well.

MOROCCAN CARROT SALAD

That old wives' tale about carrots helping you see in the dark isn't entirely off target; they're packed with betacarotene, which is an important nutrient in maintaining healthy eyes.

2 large carrots
Handful of black pitted olives
8 red radishes
Clove of garlic
Juice of 1 lemon
Clump of fresh parsley
½ tsp paprika
¼ tsp ground cumin
Pinch of cinnamon
Pinch of cayenne pepper
Shot of olive oil

PEEL and halve the carrots lengthways, thinly slice into segments and throw into a bowl.
SLICE the radishes and add to the carrots.
QUARTER the olives, chop the parsley and combine in the bowl.
WHISK the lemon juice, spices and oil together with the peeled and crushed garlic and dress the salad bits.
SERVE with mixed leaf salad and crusty bread for lunch or to accompany lamb or fish for dinner.

PASTA & RISOTTO

No rookie cookbook would dare call itself complete without a good wad of pasta and risotto dishes. Whether you're a student strapped for cash, a parent trying to find a recipe the entire family can enjoy, or wanting something quick to throw together for friends, then pasta or rice is usually a safe bet. But better than just safe ... these recipes are show stoppers.

Onlookers will suspect you've smuggled an Italian chef into your kitchen, when in actual fact you've mastered these suppers the simple way ... the SORTED way!

LEEK AND BACON RISOTTO

Dirty plates lead to rotting food, which leads to bad hygiene, which leads to death. OK, so we may have exaggerated here. But our point is that nobody enjoys the washing up . . . do they? We all want minimum effort with maximum result, and this dish does it all. Bung everything into one pot and that's your lot. Simple, wholesome food that's like a slap in the face for all those hard-core kitchen grafters.

1 large leek
Shot of olive oil
2 cloves of garlic
Bacon or gammon offcuts (750g)
Mushrooms (400g)
Risotto rice (500g)
¼ of a bottle of white wine
Chicken stock (1 litre)
Cream cheese (200g)
Handful of chopped parsley

SHRED leek and wash thoroughly.
SWEAT leek in a pan in the shot of oil with the lid on.
PEEL and crush garlic and add to leek.
REMOVE excess fat from bacon (or gammon) and cut into bite-sized pieces.
ADD to leek mix and continue to fry.
SLICE mushrooms and chuck them in.
HEAT the stock in a saucepan, or make up stock if you're using a cube.
POUR rice in and stir to evenly coat grains.
SLOSH in the wine and stir until nearly absorbed.
LADLE in the hot stock bit by bit, allowing the rice to absorb the liquid before adding more, stirring throughout until rice is plump and cooked (approximately 20 minutes).
STIR in the cream cheese and parsley and season.
SERVE in bowls – perfect for TV dinners with mates.

BEETROOT AND HORSERADISH RISOTTO WITH TROUT

We've heard that you should never trust luminous food … but we want to put an end to this rumour! The exceptions should be piccalilli and SORTED's beetroot risotto. This dish uses the classic risotto method but after including the beetroot, horseradish and Parmesan you'll have something so pink and glossy that even Barbie would be wowed.

1 small onion
2 cloves of garlic
Knob of butter
Risotto rice (200g)
White wine (200ml)
1 litre veg stock
Pack of pre-cooked beetroot, not in vinegar (250g)
Shot of olive oil
2 rainbow trout fillets, pin boned, skin on
Juice of ½ a lemon
Heaped tbsp of horseradish sauce
Chunk of Parmesan, grated
Splash of cream
1 punnet of cress, picked and washed

PEEL and dice the onion and garlic as finely as possible.
SWEAT them off gently in a saucepan with the butter for 5 minutes.
DUMP in the risotto rice and stir to coat every grain in the buttery onions.
POUR in the wine and allow to bubble gently until absorbed.
LADLE in the stock bit by bit, stirring continuously over the heat. Don't add more until the last lot has been absorbed. Continue for 10–12 minutes until the rice is plump and cooked.
DICE the drained beetroot into 1cm cubes, then add to the cooked risotto to warm through.
HEAT a dash of oil and tiny knob of butter in a frying pan, then add the trout fillets, skin side down, and season with salt and pepper.
WHEN almost cooked through squeeze over the lemon juice and turn the fillets over, removing the pan from the heat. They will continue to cook for a few minutes.
STIR the horseradish into the risotto with the Parmesan, cream and a generous pinch of salt and pepper.
WHEN you're happy the rice is tender and you have a 'relaxed' (nothing too stiff and stodgy) portion on a plate, lay a trout fillet on top and sprinkle over the cress.

ROASTED RED PEPPER AND GOAT'S CHEESE RISOTTO

When a plate of food is based around an ingredient that leaks starch you have to balance it with light and vibrant ingredients and textures to avoid stodgy results. This version, albeit a slight cheat with a blitzed-up jar of roasted peppers, sings the flavours of summer and, with the added bite and ooze from the rocket and goat's cheese, you'll have restaurant-quality risotto every time.

1 small onion
2 cloves of garlic
Knob of butter
Risotto rice (250g)
White wine (250ml)
1 litre of hot veg stock
Jar of roasted red peppers
Chunk of Parmesan, grated
Splash of cream
Handful of fresh rocket, washed
Wedge of goat's cheese

sortedfood.com/
redpepperrisotto

PEEL and chop the onion and garlic as finely as possible.
SWEAT them off gently in a saucepan with the butter for 5 minutes.
DUMP in the rice and stir to coat every grain in the buttery onions.
POUR in the wine and bubble gently until absorbed.
LADLE in the stock bit by bit, stirring continuously over the heat. Don't add more stock until the last lot has absorbed. Continue for 10–12 minutes until the rice is plump and cooked.
DRAIN the oil from the red peppers then blitz them in a food processor to form a purée.
STIR the purée into the risotto with the Parmesan, cream and a generous pinch of salt and pepper.
WHEN you're happy the rice is tender and you have a 'relaxed' texture (nothing too stiff and stodgy) then quickly pile on the rocket and divide into big bowls.
CRUMBLE over the goat's cheese and serve.

ZINGY CRAB LINGUINE

We aren't all lucky enough to have big kitchens to create incredible food in ... but that should be no excuse. Some of the greatest food doesn't need much time, equipment or space. This fresh, tantalizing pasta dish is a prime example: thrown together in the smallest of spaces and yet wouldn't look out of place in a top restaurant.

Handful of dried linguine (100g)
1 small red chilli
Clove of garlic
Couple of sprigs of fresh parsley
4 tbsp olive oil
3 tbsp lemon juice
1 tin of crab (170g), drained

PUT a large pan of salted water on to boil.
DUMP the linguine into the pan and stir to make sure the strands don't stick together, then allow to simmer for 8 minutes (or as packet instructions).
DICE the chilli (seeds as well if you like it fiery), grate the garlic and chop the parsley, adding all to a mug with the oil, lemon juice and plenty of salt and pepper.
DRAIN the pasta and return to the dry, but hot pan.
STIR through the crab meat and splash over the oil dressing.
MIX well and serve immediately.
STASH any leftovers for a pasta salad the following day.

CHICKEN, MUSHROOM AND TARRAGON PASTA BAKE

Heavy drinking sessions ...We all have to face them some time or another. Whether it's for your sports team, a society do or a birthday celebration, they're potentially devastating rituals which will make you more anxious than a pig attending a bacon convention. So save face and remember to line your stomach well beforehand. This quick pasta bake does just the job. Good old-fashioned stodgy fare, packed with the earthy flavours of mushrooms and tarragon, which will slow down alcohol absorption and make you look like a seasoned pro in the shot-slurping stakes.

Penne (400g)
Clove of garlic
Button mushrooms (150g)
Shot of olive oil
Knob of butter
2 chicken breasts
Cream of chicken and mushroom soup (400g)
Milk (100ml)
Handful of fresh tarragon
Handful of grated cheese

PREHEAT oven to 200°C.
COOK pasta in salted water according to packet instructions.
PEEL and crush the garlic.
FRY them in a little oil and the butter.
DRAIN the pasta.
CUT chicken into strips and add the mushrooms.
POUR in soup, then add 100ml of milk to the can, swirl then add to the pan.
HEAT to a simmer and cook for 5 minutes.
STIR through finely chopped tarragon once chicken is cooked.
MIX in the cooked pasta.
TURN out into ovenproof casserole dish.
SPRINKLE with grated cheese and bake for 15 minutes or until crisp and golden on top.

BEEF MEATBALLS IN TOMATO SAUCE

Minced beef is a staple in almost everyone's shopping basket. So if you're fed up of the same old spag bol or cottage pie and want to spice things up a bit then try this tasty little number, a firm family favourite with a cutting edge. A pinch or two of cupboard spices and a little kick of chilli makes these balls of beef all the more moreish.

Tomato sauce
1 large onion
3 cloves of garlic
Olive oil
2 x 400g tins of chopped tomatoes
Handful of fresh basil
Dash of balsamic vinegar

Meatballs
1 onion
4 cloves of garlic
2 large red chillies
Minced beef (approx. 1.5 kg)
2 eggs
Tbsp ground coriander
Tbsp ground cumin
Handful of fresh parsley, chopped
Tbsp salt
Vegetable or olive oil
Dried pasta, depending on how hungry you are (600g)
Parmesan or cheddar cheese, grated

PEEL and chop the onion and garlic finely for the tomato sauce and sweat in a pan with a little oil until soft.
TIP in the chopped tomatoes and simmer for 20 minutes.
CHOP the onion, garlic and chillies for the meatballs as finely as possible.
DUMP into a big bowl with the minced beef.
CRACK in the eggs and sprinkle over the spices, chopped parsley and salt.
MIX together with your hands – get stuck in.
ROLL into small balls and fry in hot oiled pan until brown on all sides.
BOIL the pasta in salted water for 10–12 minutes (see packet) and drain.
CUT the basil and add to the sauce with the vinegar, salt and pepper.
STIR the meatballs through the sauce and simmer gently for a few minutes.
SERVE mixed into the pasta with a sprinkling of cheese.

TOP TIP
How about using the same meatball mix in another way. Try forming them into burgers, as large as you dare, fry them off and slap in a bap with a sliver of cheese.

RIBBONED COURGETTE, LEMON AND BASIL TAGLIATELLE

This recipe is the epitome of pasta dishes ... minimal ingredients simply combined. Then take a step back and admire your handiwork before tucking in and demolishing the fresh bowl of amazing flavours.

2 small courgettes
Olive oil
Clove of garlic
Bunch of fresh basil
1 lemon
Dried tagliatelle (200g)

BRING a pan of salted water to the boil.

HEAT up a griddle pan.

STRIP the courgettes into long pieces using a potato peeler, discarding the very centre core.

TOSS the strips in a bowl with a glug of olive oil.

CHAR the courgette strips on the griddle, a minute or so on each side, taking care not to let them go mushy.

ADD the pasta to the boiling water and cook for 8 minutes (or as packet).

PEEL and grate the garlic and tear up the basil.

SQUEEZE the juice from the lemon and mix with the basil, garlic, a glug of oil and plenty of salt and pepper.

DRAIN the pasta when cooked and stir in the courgette strips and basil dressing.

SERVE immediately with crusty bread.

GARLIC AND THYME MUSHROOM LASAGNE

Everybody loves a good classic, and very little gets more praise around the dinner table than a lasagne. This version strips out the time-consuming ragout and jumps straight in with a vegetarian alternative. It's creamy, satisfying and the SORTED mushroom twist is sure to get the whole family salivating as it's brought bubbling to the table.

1 small onion
2 cloves of garlic
Shot of olive oil
Few sprigs of fresh thyme
Selection of different mushrooms (750g), whatever you prefer
Worcestershire sauce
2 cups of crème fraiche (500g)
16 sheets of dried lasagne
A few chives, chopped
Chunk of Parmesan cheese, grated (use vegetarian varieties if you require)

BRING a large pan of salted water to the boil.
PREHEAT the oven to 200°C.
PEEL and finely dice the onion and garlic.
FRY the onion and garlic in a shot of olive oil for 5 minutes until soft and sweet.
STRIP the thyme leaves from their stalks and add to the pan.
BRUSH any dirt from the mushrooms and roughly chop.
DUMP the mushrooms into the pan and fry for a further 5 minutes until they've darkened and softened.
SPLASH in a glug of Worcestershire sauce and the crème fraiche, warm through then mix in the chives and season, leaving a few chives to garnish.
COOK the lasagne sheets in the water for 2 minutes each (you can do 3 or 4 sheets at a time, just put them in separately so they don't stick together).
SCOOP the partially cooked sheets out of the water and leave to one side on a sheet of cling film so they don't stick to the chopping board.
LAYER the mushroom mixture, softened pasta sheets and grated Parmesan into a baking dish, making sure you have at least three layers of each and finishing off with pasta, Parmesan and a sprinkling of chopped chives.
BAKE in the oven for 20 minutes until bubbling and golden.
SERVE with garlic bread and crisp green salad.

When it comes down to it, food is fuel. Day in and day out we get home and need to fill our bellies with munch, and quickly too. As soon as the cooking part becomes a chore then the battle is lost. So club together with flatmates or friends, take it in turns and when you need a little more substance than just a light bite you can throw together these effortless meals.

Starting with the classic collision of meat and two veg we offer you our twists to bring them bang up to date. The first meals don't take any longer than peeling, chopping and boiling up a few potatoes. As usual we're taking a simple concept – mashed potato – and seeing what we can do to transform the humble spud into spud-tacular results! Not only does the meat and mash formula provide you with a nutritionally balanced meal, but by bulking out your plate with simple ingredients you can stretch a limited budget. The challenge is to make sure you never get fed up with the same old mash, and that's where we hope to inspire.

We'll also make you a dab hand with steaks – impressing like a pro when asking your guests how they'd like it cooked. In the past 'edible' may have been good enough, but now we're rocking!

Or why not something a little more multicultural . . . fajitas, chicken satay and stir-fries tick all the boxes for speedy midweek meals.

MEAT

QUICK COOKS

CLASSIC MASH

Potatoes (1kg) – russet or Maris Piper are brilliant
1 tsp salt
Mug of milk
Small knob of butter

PEEL the spuds and quarter or halve them depending on their size –
just make sure they're all roughly equal.
DUMP them into a pan and just cover with cold salted water.
BRING to the boil and simmer for 20 minutes or so.
POKE with a skewer to check they're cooked. There should be no
resistance in the centre of the potatoes – if there is you'll end up
with lumpy mash.
DRAIN and return to the dry, hot pan.
SPLASH in the milk and butter and mash well until smooth. Simple!

BANGERS AND MUSTARD MASH

Quality meaty sausages (about 12)
Beef stock (1 litre)
Tbsp Worcestershire sauce
Tbsp cornflour
Bag of frozen peas (400g)
Heaped tbsp wholegrain mustard
1 × classic mash (see page 129)
Crispy onion rings (see page 49)

£ ⌣ 40 4

PREHEAT the grill to a medium heat, approx. 200°C.
PRICK the sausages and stick them on a rack under the grill for
15 minutes, turning occasionally, until golden and cooked through.
PUT on a pan of salted water and bring to the boil ready for the peas.
HEAT up the stock in another pan and whisk in the
Worcestershire sauce.
DISSOLVE the cornflour in a small pot of cold water and pour into
the hot stock, stirring continuously. Simmer for a few minutes to thicken.
TIP the peas into the boiling water and simmer until floating –
about 2–3 minutes.
BEAT the mustard into the hot classic mash.
DRAIN the peas and serve the meal with onion rings as a mountain of
food to demolish with mates.

PORK CHOP WITH APPLE AND SAGE MASH, CIDER CREAM SAUCE AND BROCCOLI

4 hefty pork chops
Vegetable or olive oil
1 onion
2 cloves of garlic
½ a can of cider (approx. 250ml)
Head of broccoli
Double cream (100ml)
Tbsp apple sauce
Few sprigs of fresh sage, finely chopped
1 × classic mash (see page 129)

PREHEAT the grill to 'high' and stick a pan of salted water on to boil.

RUB the chops in seasoned oil and place them under the hot grill for 5–6 minutes on each side.

PEEL and dice the onion as finely as possible, peel and crush the garlic and fry with the lid on, in a dash of oil, until soft.

CRANK up the heat and pour in the cider. Let it sizzle and bubble to reduce to a syrupy consistency.

PREPARE the broccoli by cutting it into mini florets, all roughly the same size.

POUR the cream into the sauce and bring to a gentle simmer.

DUMP the broccoli into the now rapidly boiling water and cook for about 3 minutes. The florets should still be vibrant green and have a slight 'bite' when done.

BEAT the apple sauce and sage through the hot classic mash. When the pork is cooked, serve with drained broccoli, sage mash and a drizzle of cider cream sauce.

GAMMON STEAK WITH TARRAGON-BUTTERED NEW POTATOES AND SAUTÉED MUSHROOMS

New potatoes (400g), scrubbed
4 handfuls of your favourite mushrooms
Vegetable or olive oil
Knob of butter
Clove of garlic
4 gammon steaks
Handful of fresh tarragon, finely chopped
Knob of salted butter, melted

PUT a pan of cold salted water onto the stove and add the new potatoes, halving any larger than bite-size.

BRING to the boil and simmer for 12–15 minutes until the spuds are just cooked – test by poking with a small knife.

WIPE any dirt from the mushrooms and hack into thumb-sized pieces, stalks and all.

HEAT a pan for a minute or so with a shot of oil, then throw in the butter and mushrooms. Avoid moving the mushrooms too much as they cook – it's best to get a golden colour on them before shaking them about and releasing too much liquid.

PEEL and crush the garlic into the mushrooms halfway through cooking.

CUT the gammon steaks into portions and pan fry for a couple of minutes on each side.

SEASON the mushrooms when cooked with salt and plenty of black pepper.

DRAIN the potatoes and return to the dry, hot pan.

ADD the tarragon and melted butter to the potato pan and gently roll the spuds around to coat.

SERVE with the mushrooms and chunky gammon steak.

Top Tip
Use a griddle pan to cook the gammon if you've got one, to improve the end presentation.

PURE CARNIVORE

OIL YOUR MEAT
Forget about frying your steak as it swims about in gallons of oil! It's best to oil the meat itself. Season a small plate of oil with plenty of salt and pepper and rub this onto the steak just before adding it to the hot pan or grill.

HOT HOT HOT!
A hot pan is crucial. You want to sear the steak and seal in all that flavour. Anything less and it'll begin to stew in its own juices and you won't get that gorgeous caramelised flavour on the outside of the steak.

A BIT OF FAT WON'T HARM!
Fat isn't a bad thing in moderation – it keeps a healthy animal warm. But if the steak has a thick layer of fat on one side (like with a sirloin) then make sure it's well cooked. Stand the meat up on the fatty side in the pan because the crisp golden fat is much nicer and more presentable than the unbearable, anaemic and chewy alternative.

HOW WOULD YOU LIKE IT COOKED, SIR?
An approximate guide to cooking steak can be got from feeling the fleshy muscle in your palm at the base of your thumb. When the firmness of the steak resembles this muscle then it's at the 'rare' stage. Touch the tip of your thumb with your middle finger and now the same muscle resembles a steak cooked to 'medium'. Repeat the process again with the thumb touching the little finger and it'll be spot on for a 'well done' steak. See the demo on our website.

CLEAR RUNNING JUICES
Chicken must always be cooked until there is no pink flesh remaining and all the juices running out of the meat are clear. Any signs of blood and it needs a little more cooking.

SECRET TO SUCCULENT CHICKEN
If you're roasting chicken, then adding a little swig of water to the roasting tin helps to keep the meat moist and succulent, but still allows for a crispy golden skin.

GET IT RIGHT!
Pork, like chicken, is traditionally cooked right through. Take care not to overcook pork though as it can go very dry and rubbery quite quickly.

GO THE EXTRA MILE
When frying any meat, a little knob of butter added halfway through cooking will add fantastic flavour and improve the golden colour you're aiming for. Add it too soon, though, and it has the chance to burn, turn dark brown and taint the meat.

MOLTEN PLASTIC WON'T HELP ANYONE
Larger cuts of meat, like a whole chicken breast or pork chop, benefit from frying in a hot pan to start, then transferring the pan to the oven to finish them off. Just make sure the pan is ovenproof. Plastic handles are a mistake!

Time out ...
When the steak's cooked how you like it, be sure to let it rest on a warm plate for 2–3 minutes. The temperature inside has to stabilise so that any remaining blood doesn't ooze out as soon as you cut through it.

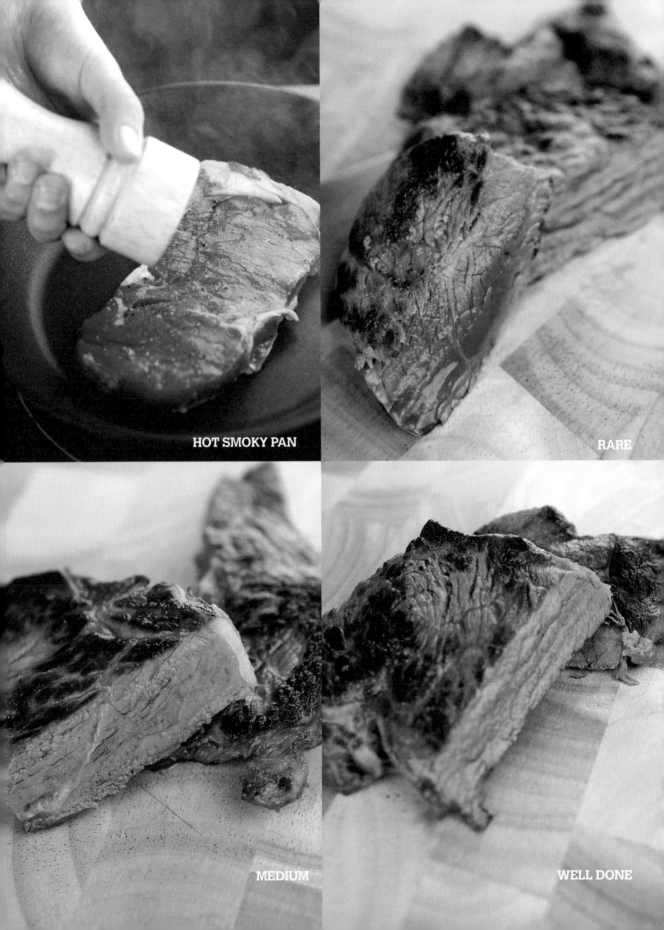

HOT SMOKY PAN

RARE

MEDIUM

WELL DONE

SIRLOIN STEAK WITH HORSERADISH DAUPHINOISE AND BAKED PORTOBELLO MUSHROOMS

4–5 large potatoes – use floury ones like King Edward
Knob of butter
2 cups of double cream (350ml)
2 tbsp creamed horseradish
4 sirloin steaks (about 200g each)
4 large portobello mushrooms
Few sprigs of fresh thyme
2 cloves of garlic
Vegetable or olive oil

PREHEAT the oven to 170°C.
PEEL the potatoes and then slice as thinly as possible.
RUB butter all over an ovenproof baking dish and layer in the potato slices, seasoning with salt and pepper between each layer. Aim for at least 5 layers.
MIX the cream and horseradish in a jug and pour over the potatoes, shaking it so the cream seeps all the way through.
BAKE in the oven for 1 hour.
CRANK up the oven to 220°C and cook for another 15 minutes.
WIPE the mushrooms clean and place them in a lidded ovenproof dish.
STRIP the leaves from the thyme and sprinkle over the mushrooms.
PEEL and grate the garlic over and dot with small bits of butter. Season well and cover with the lid.
BAKE in the hot oven next to the gratin for about 5–6 minutes.
RUB the steak in seasoned oil then fry in a very hot frying pan to seal it and give it a golden colour.
COOK the steak to personal preference (see page 136) then leave the meat to rest in a warm place for at least 3 minutes.
SERVE the steak, gratin and mushroom together with a side order of roasted vine cherry tomatoes, steamed spinach or green beans to make it perfect.

Top Tip
If you can't find a roasting dish with a suitable lid then tightly cover the dish with tin foil. It's important to keep the steam in as the mushrooms bake.

BEEF STIR-FRY

Whether you're cramming in eternal revision or ferrying yourself to and from endless commitments, you'll know that you barely have enough time to make your next Pot Noodle. However, this dish comes with Time Lord capabilities. Blast some leftover meat, veg and noodles in a wok and before you know it you'll be staring at a healthy, tasty dish fit for any mid-week meal.

Clove of garlic
1 medium onion
Thumb-sized piece of ginger
1 red pepper
½ a courgette
Handful of mangetout
Large rump or sirloin steak (200g)
Shot of vegetable oil
Medium egg noodles (150g)
Shot of soy sauce
Dollop of oyster sauce
Sesame seeds or chilli to serve

HEAT a wok or large pan on the hob and bring a small pan of salted water to the boil for the noodles.

PEEL and crush the garlic. Peel and slice the onion and ginger.

CUT the pepper, courgette, mangetout and beef into thin strips.

HEAT the oil in the wok and flash fry the beef until browned. Remove from the pan and place on a plate.

FRY all the vegetables, starting with the onion, garlic and ginger.

BOIL noodles in the salted water according to packet instructions – usually 3–4 minutes.

RETURN the beef to the wok with the soy sauce and oyster sauce and drained noodles.

TOSS everything well before serving with a sprinkling of toasted sesame seeds or finely sliced chilli.

CHICKEN AND BLACK PUDDING WITH COLCANNON

4 chicken breasts
Olive or vegetable oil
Head of Savoy cabbage
1 onion
Black pudding sausage (200g)
1 × classic mash (see page 129)
Knob of butter

PREHEAT the oven to 200°C.

RUB the chicken breasts in seasoned oil and lay them on a baking tray.

POUR over a little water and bake in the oven for 15–20 minutes.

PEEL off the outside leaves of the cabbage, cut into quarters and remove the tough centre stalk. Finely shred the cabbage with a knife.

PEEL and dice the onion and fry it with a dash of oil in a saucepan, then add the cabbage and cook for a few minutes.

REMOVE the plastic casing from the black pudding and slice into rounds. Fry in a hot pan for a few minutes so it is crisp outside but still soft inside.

BEAT the cooked onion and cabbage (which should still be nice and green) into the hot classic mash to make your colcannon and add a little more butter.

BALANCE the chicken and black pudding on top of the colcannon to serve.

SKEWERED PAPRIKA CHICKEN WITH OREGANO-ROASTED NEW POTATOES AND CRISP SALAD

This is a fantastic recipe for a barbecue, but almost as good on a grill, or even in a very hot oven. Make sure you soak the wooden skewers in water for 30 minutes so they don't catch fire!

New potatoes (400g)
Olive oil
Few sprigs of fresh oregano, leaves stripped (or use dried)
4 chicken breasts
Juice of 1 lemon
Smoked paprika
Pinch of salt
Crisp mixed-leaf salad and dressing
8 metal or wooden skewers

PREHEAT the oven to 200°C. If using wooden skewers soak in water for 30 minutes.

PUT the new potatoes in a baking tray and drizzle with a glug of olive oil, salt, pepper and the oregano.

ROLL the potatoes around to evenly coat them and roast in the oven for 40 minutes.

TRIM the chicken and slice the meat into thin strips.

POUR a shot of olive oil and the lemon juice into a dish large enough for the meat, and add a sprinkle of smoked paprika and a pinch of salt.

WHISK to combine well, then add the chicken and turn to cover it all in the marinade.

PREHEAT the grill to its hottest setting. If you don't have a separate grill then wait for the potatoes to finish, cover the tray in tin foil to keep warm, and use the oven for the chicken.

THREAD the strips of chicken onto the skewers and grill, roast or barbecue to char the outside but leave the inside succulent (this takes roughly 6 to 7 minutes, turning occasionally).

SERVE the skewers straight from the grill with the roasted new potatoes and salad tossed in your chosen dressing from the fridge.

DIY CHICKEN FAJITAS

Whether you're reading this from your university halls of residence and wondering how to get the most use out of your shared kitchen, or if you're at home wanting to get your children more involved in cooking their tea, this recipe for DIY fajitas is a great way to bring everyone together. With hardly any skill involved, the idea is simple: drum up this range of different fillings, lay 'em on the table and share the love!

2 chicken breasts
1 yellow pepper
1 red pepper
1 large onion
Cajun spice mix (30g sachet)
8 flour tortilla wraps
1 pot each of salsa, guacamole (see page 50) and sour cream
Bowl of crisp salad leaves

TRIM and slice the chicken as thinly as possible.
SLICE and de-seed the peppers.
PEEL and slice the onion and fry with the chicken in a large saucepan or wok over very high heat for 5 minutes.
ADD the peppers and continue to fry for another 5 minutes.
SPRINKLE over the Cajun spice mix and toss together.
WARM the tortillas in the microwave for a few seconds.
LAY out all the fillings on the table and dive in to make your own before everyone beats you to it.

Top Tip
Eating fajitas can get messy. Best to pile the food into the centre of the wrap then turn up the bottom before folding in each side.

CRUNCHY, CREAMY CHICKEN SATAY

What better way to kick off the barbecue season than with these fancy little satay sticks. Chuck them on the barbie, rustle up the sauce and serve with salad or rice.

4 chicken breasts
Vegetable or olive oil
3 tbsp balti curry paste
1 large onion
3 cloves of garlic
Jar of crunchy peanut butter (250g)
Tin of coconut milk (400g)
White rice (300g)
Handful of fresh coriander

sortedfood.com/
chickensatay

LIGHT your barbie or preheat the grill to its highest setting. If using wooden skewers, soak in water for 30 minutes.

CUBE the chicken into 2–3cm chunks and rub with oil and curry paste, leaving to marinate for a while.

PEEL and finely chop the onion and garlic and fry in a saucepan with a shot of vegetable oil until soft and sweet.

THREAD the chicken pieces onto 8 skewers and stack on a plate.

SCOOP the peanut butter out of its jar and add to the onions with the coconut milk and the remainder of the marinade. Combine and simmer gently until it starts to thicken.

COOK the rice in a large pan of salted water as per packet instructions until light and fluffy.

GRILL the skewers under the hot grill or on the barbecue for about 6–7 minutes minutes, turning occasionally.

DRAIN the rice and pile onto a large serving dish, top with the skewers and ladle over the sauce.

SPRINKLE with freshly chopped coriander.

MEAT

SLOW COOKS

If it's buckets of flavour and sumptuous meat you're after, then these next few pages are for you. We reveal the secrets to some awesome dishes with such deep, rich and satisfying flavours that you won't believe how straightforward they are.

You'll only spend a handful of minutes in the kitchen, after which you can just love it and leave it to do its thing – simmering and bubbling away, becoming tastier by the minute while you chill out and do . . . well, whatever it is you do to chill out. No babysitting required!

It's the cheaper cuts of meat that work best here, but they'll need slow, gentle cooking to tenderise the meat and release its magic into the dish. Dinner will be ready when you are – for once you've got the control. If you want to delay mealtime until the decisive moment of that must-see soap, then it can wait. Another 20 minutes in the oven will only do good!

BEST CUTS OF MEAT
These are the best choices for slow cooking. They have the most flavour.

LEG

THIGH

SHIN

SHOULDER

BEEF AND GUINNESS STEW WITH HORSERADISH DUMPLINGS

Stew
2 large onions
3 carrots
3 sticks of celery
Double shot of vegetable oil
Heaped tbsp tomato purée
Tbsp plain flour
Can of Guinness (440ml)
Beef stock (250ml)
Diced shin of beef (1kg)
3 cloves of garlic
2 bay leaves
Sprig of fresh thyme

Dumplings
Beef suet (150g)
Self-raising flour (150g)
2 tbsp horseradish sauce
Water to bind

sortedfood.com/
beefandalestew

PREHEAT the oven to 160°C.
PEEL and chop onions, carrots and celery into thumb-sized pieces.
DUMP into a large casserole pan with the oil and fry over a high heat, allowing the veg to brown and scraping up the browned bits from the bottom of the pan as you go.
ADD the tomato purée and flour once the vegetables are coloured, stirring until the flour is all mixed in.
POUR the Guinness into the casserole, followed by the beef stock.
BRING up to a gentle simmer and add the beef to the casserole.
PEEL and finely chop the garlic and add along with the bay leaves and thyme. Season with salt and pepper.
COVER the casserole with a lid and place in the preheated oven to cook for 2–3 hours, checking occasionally to stir and make sure the side isn't catching and burning.
PLACE the suet in a bowl and sift in the flour. Mix well, then season with salt, freshly ground black pepper and horseradish sauce.
CREATE a 'well' in the centre of the mixture and add water a bit at a time.
MIX with your hands until you get a firm dough that comes away cleanly from the sides of the bowl.
TURN out the dough onto a clean board and sprinkle over some flour.
ROLL the dough out into a sausage shape, then divide and form into 10 golf-ball sized dumplings (they'll double in size when cooking).
DROP the dumplings carefully into the stew for the last half an hour of cooking. You'll know when the beef's done because it will almost fall apart when touched. The dumplings should be light and fluffy.
SERVE the dumplings and beef stew in large bowls with fresh veg.

BEEF RENDANG CURRY AND AROMATIC RICE

Stewing beef is one of the most popular cuts of meat for slow-cooking methods. Of course, this rendang is not as common in the UK as beef in ale or beef in red wine, and that's what SORTED loves about it. Something a little bit different and exciting but using the same methods and techniques. This tasty Indonesian dish hits the spot every time!

For the rendang	Aromatic rice
1 onion	Basmati rice (300g)
Thumb-sized piece of fresh ginger	5 cardamom pods
3 cloves of garlic	1 cinnamon stick
2 red chillies	Tsp salt
Stick of lemon grass	Handful of fresh coriander
Zest and juice of 1 lime	
Tsp cinnamon	
Tsp turmeric	
Tsp salt	
Stewing beef (750g)	
Shot of vegetable oil	
Tin of coconut milk (400ml)	
Handful of desiccated coconut	

PREHEAT the oven to 160°C.

PEEL the onion, ginger and garlic and chop roughly.

THROW them into a blender with the chillies, lemon grass, lime zest, spices and salt and blitz to a paste.

LOOSEN it up with the lime juice and a splash of water if needed.

SLICE the beef into cubes and fry in the oil in an ovenproof pan for a couple of minutes to colour.

SPOON in the aromatic paste and fry for another 2 minutes, then pour in the coconut milk.

TOAST the desiccated coconut in a dry pan until golden and tip into the rendang mix.

PLACE the pan in the preheated oven and cook for an hour with the lid on and an additional half an hour without the lid, until most of the liquid has evaporated and what is left is a dark and rich curry-style dish.

WASH the rice in the meantime to remove any excess starch and leave to drain.

With 25 minutes to go ...

TRANSFER the rice to a pan with the cardamom pods, cinnamon stick, 750ml of water and the salt, then bring to the boil.

SIMMER until most of the water has been absorbed, then put on a lid and after about 30 seconds remove the pan from the heat.

LEAVE the rice to rest for 10 minutes or so, and you'll end up with perfectly cooked and fluffy grains.

CHOP the fresh coriander and mix through the rice as you serve it with the beef rendang.

BEEF AND SPINACH CURRY

Jesus fed the five thousand with five loaves of bread and two fish. If only he'd known about our beef and spinach curry! It's a dish of biblical proportions, filling enough to satisfy the most famished of paupers – no mean feat. This is no-nonsense nosh which screams out simplicity and is as cheap as chips. It's great for absorbing the alcohol after that 'quiet drink' at the pub that turned into a marathon session. Or simply a quality, sociable meal for you and your mates.

2 large onions
2 cloves of garlic
Thumb-sized piece of fresh ginger
Shot of olive oil
Beef stewing steak (1kg)
Tbsp ground cumin
Tsp ground turmeric
Tbsp chilli powder
Tbsp salt
Tin of chopped tomatoes (400g)
Spinach, fresh or frozen (400g)
8 cardamom pods
2 tbsp plain yoghurt
Naan breads

PREHEAT the oven to 180°C.
PEEL and finely chop the onion, garlic and ginger and fry in the oil in a large ovenproof saucepan until soft.
CUBE the stewing steak, removing any sinew or gristle.
ADD to the hot pan and sear the meat.
ADD the spices and stir well.
TIP in the tomatoes and spinach and bring to the boil, stirring to break up the spinach.
COVER with a lid and cook in the oven for 3 hours.
REMOVE the lid for the last half hour to get the desired consistency.
SERVE with a dollop of yoghurt, baked naan breads and ice-cold lager!

TOP TIP
Do the preparation and bung it in the oven, then wander down the bar for a game of pool and a pint or two before heading home to the perfect end to any night – a quality Ruby Murray.

LAMB AND APRICOT TAGINE WITH SPICED COUSCOUS

Tagine might sound exotic, but honestly, it's just a fancy name for a rich and aromatic stew that originates from North Africa. It's another brilliant way of using tougher and cheaper cuts of meat and transforming them into succulent mouth-watering meals. The lamb works particularly well with the sweetness of the apricots, cinnamon and almonds in SORTED's twist on this classic Moroccan dish.

For the tagine
2 large onions
Shot of olive oil
Tbsp ground cumin
Tbsp ground coriander
Tbsp ground cinnamon
3 cloves of garlic
Lamb leg or shoulder, boned, trimmed and diced (1kg)
Lamb or veg stock (400ml)
2 tbsp honey
Juice of 1 small lemon
5–6 fresh tomatoes
2 handfuls of dried apricots
Handful of flaked almonds

For the couscous
Couscous (200g)
Handful of Sultanas
Tsp salt
Tsp turmeric
Couple of spring onions
Glug of olive oil
Handful of fresh coriander

sortedfood.com/ lambtagine

PREHEAT the oven to 160°C.
PEEL and slice the onions, then fry them in the oil in an ovenproof saucepan for 5 minutes.
SPOON the dried spices into the onions with the peeled and crushed garlic, season well with salt and pepper and cook for a minute.
TIP the diced lamb into the pan, cover with the stock and add the honey and lemon juice.
HACK up the tomatoes and put all the flesh, seeds and juice in the pan.
BRING the mixture to a gentle simmer, cover with a lid and place it in the preheated oven for 1 hour.
ADD the apricots and stir the tagine well. Return to the oven for another 30 minutes without the lid.
POUR the couscous in a measuring jug to work out its volume, then pour into a bowl with the sultanas, salt, turmeric and the finely sliced spring onions.
MEASURE the same volume of boiling water and pour into the couscous, stir, then cover with a plate or lid for 3 minutes.
TOAST the almonds in a dry pan until golden all over and garnish the tagine with them.
FLUFF up the couscous with a fork and mix in the olive oil and finely chopped fresh coriander.
SERVE the tagine with the couscous.

WHERE ALL GREAT
IDEAS ARE BORN . . .
THE PUB!

CHICKEN AND LEEK PIE

Similar pies can be found scattered across pub menus up and down the country – with good reason: they taste great. But none is as satisfying as the one you make yourself. The beauty of it is that once you have the know-how you can make the fillings as humble or as sophisticated as you like. Some might argue that life's too short to make your own pastry, so for this recipe we've cheated and used ready-made. This recipe can make one large family-sized pie or four individual ones.

Cider (500ml)
2 carrots
2 bay leaves
3 leeks
4 chicken breasts, sinew and fat removed
Butter (50g)
Plain flour (50g)
Milk (200ml)
Tsp wholegrain mustard
Ready-made puff pastry (320g)
1 egg

POUR the cider into a saucepan and bring to the boil.

PEEL and slice the carrots, add them to the cider with the bay leaves and simmer for 5 minutes.

HALVE the leeks lengthways and slice fairly thinly, then dump them into a colander and wash well to get rid of any mud or grit.

ADD the washed leeks to the simmering cider with the whole chicken breasts and cover with a lid. Simmer for about 15 minutes.

STRAIN the contents of the pan through a sieve, collecting all the liquid in a bowl.

TEAR the cooked chicken into strips when it's cool enough to handle.

MELT the butter in the now empty pan and stir in the flour. Add the strained liquid a bit at a time over a high heat, stirring continuously until a smooth paste forms. Add as much milk as you need to make a sauce the consistency of custard.

TIP the cooked chicken, carrots and leeks into the sauce, mix in the mustard and season well with salt and pepper. Pour everything into an ovenproof dish.

ROLL out the puff pastry on a lightly floured surface to the thickness of a pound coin.

BRUSH the edges of the pie dish with milk or beaten egg, then drape the rolled pastry over.

PRESS the edges against the dish to stick, then cut away any excess.

BRUSH over all the pastry with beaten egg. This makes the pastry go golden brown and look the business.

POKE a hole in the pastry lid to let the steam out when cooking.

BAKE the pie for 25–30 minutes then serve with vegetables and some mashed spuds.

CHICKEN, FENNEL AND THYME CASSEROLE

Barry's philosophy in life is to 'look good . . . then the rest will follow.' He's preached it well and all of us at SORTED are beginning to believe it. After all, you are what you eat. Eat a pizza seven days a week and you'll have a face like one. Let's see you on the pull now . . . being able to cut shapes on the dance floor like John Travolta is no good if you need to wipe down every five minutes. Save face and do the groundwork to avoid this by eating well. The fennel in this idiot-proof dish is apparently brilliant for skin, containing active spot-preventing agents.

2 handfuls of new potatoes
2 cloves of garlic
Few sprigs of fresh thyme
Shot of olive oil
2 chicken breasts
Bulb of fennel
1 courgette
1 red onion
White wine (250ml)
1 lemon
Knob of butter

PREHEAT the oven to 200°C.
WASH the new potatoes and boil them in salted water for 12–15 minutes.
PEEL and crush the garlic into a roasting tray and add the thyme before drizzling with oil.
RUB seasoned oil into the chicken breasts and lay them in the tray.
HALVE the fennel and then cut each half into thirds.
QUARTER the courgette lengthways, then cut into chunks.
PEEL and chop the red onion into wedges.
SCATTER the chopped vegetables around the chicken.
LUBRICATE all the ingredients in oil and roast for 15 minutes.
CRANK up the temperature as high as it will go and slosh the wine and lemon juice into the tray.
ROAST for a further 15 minutes and serve with buttered new potatoes.

RUSTIC BEAN AND SAUSAGE STEW

Sausage suppers have to be the ultimate comfort food, especially during miserable winter evenings. What's more, this stew really is as quick as a takeaway, half the price and with a fraction of the calories. It was one of the first meals I ever cooked for the lads when brainstorming ideas for the first book, and still crops up from time to time whenever we want proper comfort food.

8 decent-sized sausages
Shot of olive oil
1 onion
1–2 carrots
3 cloves of garlic
1 stick of celery
Tsp fresh or dried oregano
3 different 400g tins of beans, eg kidney, butter, haricot
Tin of chopped tomatoes (400g)
Handful of fresh parsley

GRILL the sausages under a high heat until golden.
PEEL and dice the onion, carrot and garlic, dice the celery and fry in oil in a large pan for 10 minutes.
DRAIN and rinse the beans and add to the pan along with the tomatoes and oregano.
CHOP the cooked sausages into chunks and stir into the bean mix.
SIMMER for 10 minutes.
SPRINKLE with the chopped parsley just before serving.

PULLED PORK AND PICKLED SLAW TACOS

Spit-roast pork is an incredible experience – meat that literally falls apart in your hands and tastes so good you wish you were back in medieval times, gorging on it day in and day out. This oven-braised version recreates that incredible encounter with slow-cooked pig and adds even more flavours for your taste buds to get excited about.

Pulled pork
Shoulder of pork (1kg)
Tsp ground cumin
Tsp smoked paprika
3 tbsp tomato ketchup
2 tbsp white wine vinegar
2 onions
2 bay leaves
Handful of fresh oregano
Juice of 1 orange

To serve
8 small corn tacos
Iceberg lettuce, shredded
Dollop of sour cream
1 red chilli, thinly sliced

Pickled slaw
½ a red cabbage
2 small carrots
Bunch of fresh coriander, chopped
Tbsp caster sugar
Juice of 1 lime
2 tbsp white wine vinegar

PREHEAT the oven to 150°C.
CUT as much fat off the shoulder of pork as you can.
RUB the meat with the cumin, paprika and ketchup.
PUT it into a large saucepan that has a tight-fitting lid.
PEEL and slice the onions.
ADD to the pan with all the other pulled-pork ingredients and a splash of water.
PUT the lid on the pan and cook in the oven for 2 hours.
SHRED the cabbage as finely as you can and dump into a big bowl.
PEEL and grate the carrot and add to the cabbage with the coriander.
MIX the sugar, lime juice and vinegar in a cup, season with salt and pepper and pour over the slaw mix to combine.
REMOVE the shoulder from the pan after the 2 hours are up and put to one side.
PUT the pan on the hob and reduce the liquid by at least half until it has a syrupy consistency.
TAKE the fat off the shoulder and discard.
PULL the rest of the pork into strips using two forks . . . it should fall apart.
POUR the syrupy juices back over the pulled pork.
SERVE the warm pork with a little of the crispy shredded lettuce, pickled slaw and a dollop of the sour cream, with optional chilli, all piled into a corn taco. Best served with a Mexican beer.

We couldn't possibly forget our slippery fishy friends, and this chapter is devoted to making the most of white fish, oily fish, whole fish, seafood and even the tinned stuff. We delved to the bottom of our deepest oceans and fastest rivers to find Nemo and his friends, and then we went one step beyond ... to come up with tasty recipes for them!

The dishes scattered through the next few pages, made for all occasions, go some way to squash the idea that fish is fancy food and best left to pros. From stews and pies, to salads and sushi we're finding it easier and easier to get rookies cooking with fish. Below you'll find schools of fresh, nutritious ideas to get you, your mates and even Captain Birdseye SORTED!

FISH

LIGHT AND FRAGRANT FISH STEW

A fantastic dish, which by definition is a stew, although one that is relatively quick to make. Yes, it needs gentle cooking, but for not nearly as long and it's done on top of the stove. And the sneaky little tip of using the garlic mayo to thicken the stew gives the dish a unique twist.

For the stew	Mayonnaise
A few strands of saffron	1 egg
1 leek	Tbsp lemon juice
1 head of fennel	Clove of garlic
Shot of olive oil	Olive oil (100ml)
Small new potatoes (500g)	
Fish stock (600ml)	
Mixed fish fillets (500g)	
Zest of ½ an orange	
Selection of other seafood – squid, raw king prawns, scallops, mussels, clams (about 250g in total)	
Bunch of chervil or flat-leaf parsley	

MAKE the mayo by cracking the egg into a blender with the lemon juice and the peeled and crushed garlic clove, then blitz.

DRIZZLE the oil into the blender slowly while it's spinning (be careful) until you get the consistency of mayonnaise. (You can make the mayo by hand using a whisk but it takes a little longer!) Season and leave the mayo to one side for later.

STICK the saffron strands into a cup, pour in a little boiling water and leave to infuse.

WASH and finely slice the leek and rinse in a colander to get rid of any mud or grit.

WASH and finely slice the fennel, then fry it gently in a large pan with the leek and olive oil, covered with a lid so that they soften without gaining colour, about 3–4 minutes.

SCRUB the potatoes clean and cut them in half.

POUR the fish stock in with the fennel and leeks and add the potatoes.

SIMMER for 10 minutes, until the potatoes are almost cooked.

SKIN and de-bone the fish and cut it into matchbox-sized pieces (see page 188).

SCATTER the orange zest into the pan along with the saffron and the infused water and stir well.

PUT the fish into the pan and poach, with the liquid just under boiling point, for about 2 minutes, then add the seafood selection and poach for a further 2–3 minutes.

CHOP the herbs and mix these in at the last moment.

FINISH the stew by stirring through some of the garlic mayo. This will thicken the soup and give it a luxurious silky feel. Don't boil the stew after adding the mayo.

ADJUST the seasoning with salt and pepper and serve with some crusty bread.

CHEAT'S FISH PIE

Cooking a pie might sound like hard work, but we've created some clever shortcuts to this usually costly and time-consuming dish. You don't have to be Delia to make this one: the seafood chowder acts as a great ready-made sauce, while that stale loaf in your cupboard will make a quality substitute for mashed potato and crisp up a treat. Carefully slide out of the oven when golden and splodge onto a plate for your savagely hungry friends and family.

6 eggs
1 large onion
Shot of olive oil
2 x 400g tins of seafood chowder
White fish fillets (800g)
2 large handfuls of fresh spinach
¾ of a loaf of stale white bread
Large knob of butter, melted

BOIL the eggs for 6–7 minutes then cool them under cold running water.
PEEL and dice the onion finely and sweat in a little oil in a large saucepan until soft.
ADD the chowder and heat through.
SKIN, pin-bone and roughly chop the fish fillets into large pieces (see page 188).
WASH the spinach and add to the soup with the fish.
SHELL and halve the eggs and stir in.
REMOVE the crusts from the bread and cube it.
POUR the contents of the pan into an ovenproof dish and top with the chopped bread.
BRUSH evenly with melted butter and bake at 180°C until crisp and golden.

NOTE
Sweet potato chips are
tricky to get crispy without
a mega hot oven, but they
taste darn good regardless.

CAJUN SPICED SALMON, MANGO SALSA AND SWEET POTATO CHIPS

SAD, Seasonal Affective Disorder, is depression caused by our long, dark winters. If you find anyone in this state, please consult this dish: it's so charismatic, cheerful and chirpy it looks like it's come singing and dancing straight from the Caribbean – an extremely useful culinary weapon to rustle up next time your mate says they're staying in cos of winter blues. SORTED food can, and will, put a smile on their face … especially if they share the cooking bit too!

2 large sweet potatoes
Shot of olive oil
4 fresh salmon fillets
Cajun spice mix
1 mango
2 spring onions
3 tomatoes
½ a red onion
Handful of fresh coriander
Fresh red chilli
2 limes

PREHEAT the oven to 200°C.
CUT potatoes into chunky slices (leave the skin on).
TOSS into a baking tray with the oil, season with salt and pepper and roast for 30 minutes.
DUST salmon with Cajun spice mix, rub into the flesh and leave to marinate.
PEEL mango and roughly chop with the spring onions, tomatoes, red onion and coriander.
COMBINE all the chopped ingredients with the finely diced chilli and juice of one of the limes.
LEAVE the mango salsa on the side while the rest of the meal cooks.
PUSH the wedges to one side of the tray and slap the salmon fillets on the other.
RETURN to the oven for 15 minutes or so until the salmon is cooked (the flesh has just turned opaque).
PILE the salsa onto plates, top each with a salmon fillet and wedge of lime and serve with sweet potato chips.

THAI-STYLE TUNA BURGERS

The human body is a fine machine but there is some stuff we still can't make … essential fatty acids, found in abundance in all oily fish, being one example. This cheap and easy burger is high in omega-3 oils (fresh tuna is chocka with these, but tinned is cheaper). You'll need them to kick start your metabolism and get your body into gear. What's even better, it'll taste like it's from the greasy spoon café but without the guilt trip. Quality grub for sharing with friends.

For the burgers
1 x 180g tin of tuna (in brine)
1 lime
Tsp finely chopped chilli
Tsp chopped fresh ginger
Bunch of fresh coriander, finely chopped
1 egg
Dusting of flour
Shot of olive oil

To serve
2 pitta breads
Mayonnaise
Handful of mixed salad leaves
Sweet chilli sauce

SQUEEZE out as much brine as possible from the tuna and put into a bowl.
ZEST the lime into the bowl with the finely chopped chilli, ginger and coriander.
CRACK in the egg and mix it up, then shape into 4 burgers.
DUST the burgers with flour, heat 1cm of oil until very hot, then fry till crisp, golden and hot right through.
WARM the pitta breads in a toaster, cut into halves and open pockets.
SPREAD on mayonnaise, chuck in salad leaves, slot in a burger and top it off with chilli sauce to dip.
STUFF your face and enjoy.

SIMPLE SUSHI

If you're a fan of rolling and shaping plasticine, then sushi is the one for you, a dish that you really can 'play' with as you cook! It's a light, healthy and delicious meal to snack on at any time. It's expensive to buy, so make it yourself and you can easily throw together rolls of the stuff to enjoy with friends. Our version avoids raw fish too, so everybody can enjoy it.

Sushi rice (250g)
Tsp salt
Tbsp caster sugar
Tbsp rice wine vinegar
Tbsp mirin (Japanese rice wine)

sortedfood.com/
sushi

Fillings
Handful of cooked prawns
6 seafood sticks
Handful of smoked salmon offcuts
1 avocado
Bunch of spring onions

6 nori sheets
Wasabi paste
Soy sauce
Fresh or pickled ginger
½ a cucumber

WASH the rice under cold running water, cook according to packet instructions. Add the salt, sugar, vinegar and mirin once cooked and cooling down. Mix well.

TRANSFER to a bowl and allow to cool.

PREPARE all the fillings by cutting into thin strips.

LAY a nori sheet on the work surface (or sushi mat) and flick a small amount of water onto it.

SPREAD cooled rice over the sheet to a thickness of 1cm. Leave a small margin at the sides.

BRUSH a little wasabi paste over the rice. Take care – it's hot stuff! If in doubt, taste a little first.

ARRANGE your fillings in a line. Ensure all the ingredients appear all the way along the sheet because it will be cut.

ROLL the sheet up tightly and dampen the end to stick it down.

WRAP in cling film and store in the fridge until required.

SLICE into 3cm pieces with a damp knife and serve with chopsticks and soy sauce, pickled ginger and wasabi.

GRILLED FISH SALAD

This superhero snacky lunch with brain-awakening qualities will have you flying through whatever new project your boss throws at you. The combination of oily fish, egg, leafy greens and potatoes helps to fuel the brain, that demanding organ which uses 30 per cent of the body's daily calories and nutrients. Keep it pumped up and ready for action.

4 new potatoes
1 egg
1 tomato
6 black pitted olives
Vinaigrette
Handful of spinach and watercress salad
2 trout fillets
½ a lemon

PREPARING THE FISH
REMOVE any excess scales by rubbing the back of a knife along the fish from the tail to the head.
SNIP off the fins from the side and back of the fish.
CUT through to the backbone of the fish, just behind its head. The closer you get, the less good fish you waste.
TURN the knife towards the tail and run it along the body right to the tail to remove one of the fillets. Feel the knife scraping along the backbone – again, this avoids leaving flesh on the bone. Flip the fish over and repeat the process on the other side to leave just the skeleton.
RUN the knife under the ribcage of each fillet to remove all of the little bones in one clean slice. Trim any excess fatty flesh away to tidy up the fillet.
SLIDE your finger gently along the centre of the fillet and you'll feel some very small bones. Pluck these out with a pair of tweezers to leave you fish fillets ready for cooking (pin-boning).

Your fish is now ready to cook!

BOIL the potatoes in a pan of salted water for 8 minutes.
DROP the egg into the same pan for a further 6 minutes.
COOL both the potatoes and egg under cold running water.
PREHEAT the grill to highest heat.
QUARTER the tomato, potatoes, olives and peeled egg.
DRESS the salad leaves, potatoes and olives in vinaigrette.
ARRANGE the eggs and tomatoes on a plate.
SEASON the fish.
GRILL the fillets for 2–3 minutes.
LAY the fillets on the salad bed and squeeze the lemon over the fish.

BAKED TROUT ON SMASHED CELERIAC AND FENNEL WITH ROASTED ROOTS

2 carrots
2 parsnips
4 shallots
Olive oil
1 celeriac
1 head of fennel
1 × classic mash (substituting celeriac and fennel for half the potato) (see page 129)
2 whole trout
Juice of 1 lemon

PREHEAT the oven to 200°C.

PEEL the carrots, parsnips and shallots.

HALVE the shallots and cut the carrots and parsnips into finger-sized chunks.

RUB them all in a little seasoned olive oil and roast on a tray in the oven for about half an hour.

CUT away the skin from the celeriac and chop into chunks the same size as the potatoes for the mash.

REMOVE the root then slice the fennel.

SUBSTITUTE fennel and celeriac for half of the potato in the classic mash and continue as per mash instructions (see page 129).

FILLET, pin-bone and trim the fish into portions, and bung them on a baking tray (see page 188).

SQUEEZE over the lemon and season with salt and pepper.

BAKE in the preheated oven for the last 8–10 minutes of the roasted vegetable cooking time, until just cooked.

SERVE the fish immediately with the roasted veg and the creamy celeriac and fennel mash.

PAN-FRIED COD ON GARLIC AND BASIL MASH, WITH ROASTED VINE TOMATOES

Cherry tomatoes on the vine (about 24)
3 cloves of garlic
Olive oil
4 portions of cod (skin on)
Plain flour
Butter
1 × classic mash cooked with 3 cloves of garlic
in the cooking water (see page 129)
Handful of fresh basil
Flavoured butter (optional, see below)

PREHEAT the oven to 200°C.

CUT the vines into portions with about 5–6 tomatoes on each.

LAY them on a baking tray with the garlic cloves from the potato water, drizzle with oil, season with salt and pepper and roast in the preheated oven until they just begin to burst.

DUST the skin of the cod with seasoned flour and fry skin-side down in hot oil with a knob of butter, until golden and crisp. Turn over for the last minute or so to complete the cooking.

MASH the garlic into the potatoes when they are cooked.

CHOP the basil fairly roughly with a sharp knife so as not to bruise the leaves and beat into the mash.

SERVE with some flavoured butter if you have any in the fridge (see page 197).

FLAVOURED BUTTER

If you're ever left with half a pack of fresh herbs without a home, or you see some on special offer, why not create a flavoured butter? You could also use crushed garlic, chilli flakes, citrus zest or toasted spices instead.

For something last minute but delicious, make up a selection of flavoured butters and stash them in the fridge until you need them. Then in a second you can sex up even the simplest piece of meat or fish.

SOFTEN some butter slightly in a microwave and finely chop the herbs.
MIX them together and spoon onto a stretch of cling film.
ROLL into a sausage shape and store in the fridge for up to two weeks.
ADD a slice to finish sauces, enrich soups or garnish steaks and fish.

Varieties
Unsalted butter (250g), with any of the following:
– 1 tsp of dried chilli flakes and 2 tsp of smoked paprika
– Finely grated zest of 3 limes and 2 tbsp of chopped fresh coriander
– 125g Roquefort cheese mashed up and 2 tbsp chopped fresh chives

MOULES MARINIÈRES

Want a reminder of the ultimate holiday food without the expense of the euro? Then make this classic French fast food!

Fresh mussels in shells (500g)
1 onion
Knob of butter
3 cloves of garlic
Glass of white wine
Juice of 1 lemon
Handful of fresh parsley, chopped
Black pepper
Splash of cream
Baguette or other crusty French bread to serve

sortedfood.com/
mussels

CLEAN the mussels by removing any excessive 'beard' and leave them to soak in water for 10 minutes.

DISCARD any that are open and don't close when tapped – they are already dead!

PEEL and dice the onion as finely as possible and sweat off with the butter in a deep-sided pan with lid.

PEEL and crush the garlic and add this to the onions halfway through the cooking time.

POUR in the white wine, squeeze in the lemon juice and dump in the drained and cleaned mussels.

COVER with the lid and leave to steam for 2–3 minutes until the mussels have all opened.

SCOOP the cooked mussels into a deep serving bowl, then add the parsley, a pinch of black pepper and cream to the cooking juices in the pan.

STIR, reduce a little if needed, and pour over the mussels.

SERVE with chunks of crusty French bread to mop up all the juices.

SWEET TREATS

It doesn't matter where the biscuit barrel is hidden, we all seem to have a sixth sense that tells us exactly where it is, what's in it and how many there are! Denial merely makes the sugar cramps more acute. Until the last single chocolate chip from the last single chocolate chip cookie is gone you just can't relax. So go on – find the little critter and eat it!

Why is there so much shame associated with this guilty pleasure?

Well, 'I made them myself' puts a completely different spin on it (bear with us). It's one thing entirely if you buy biscuits from the corner shop and scoff them all – that's plain lazy and for couch potatoes only. Instead, cooking your own cakes, cookies and tarts takes focus, precision and skill, and you are creating something for your mates and for those elusive moments when you deserve a treat.

So now we've got that straight let's get cracking. These beauties are actually pretty straightforward to make, with bog-standard cupboard ingredients that will keep for ages.

BAKING TIPS

KEEP YOUR HANDS COOL!
Working with pastry can be a delicate procedure and the dough doesn't really appreciate excessive treatment from hot hands. Limit the time you spend manoeuvring the dough, and run your hands under cold running water then dry them quickly before handling it.

IS IT NEARLY DONE YET?
Every oven will operate in its own way so the cooking times in the recipes are approximate. Always check the cake's done before taking it out. An under-cooked cake will sink in the middle as it cools and be stodgy to eat, while over-cooking will result in a dry sponge that needs a glass of milk to stop you choking on the crumbs. A simple solution is to stick a clean skewer or cocktail stick into the centre of the cake and pull it back out slowly. If it's clean the cake is done, but if any gooey mix can be seen on the skewer give it a little longer.

THE FINISHING TOUCHES
A great cake or cookie can be transformed into a stunning work of art with a little extra attention. Slicing a basic sponge in two and wedging it back together with cream and jam is always a favourite. Or why not try one of these two straightforward icings:

Glacé icing – nothing more than sieved icing sugar slowly bound together with a drop or two of cold water. Try and sex it up with some food colouring or extra liquid flavouring. Then add a tiny bit of water at a time – you'll be surprised how little it needs. Carefully spread it around and leave to set.

Butter icing – beat together twice as much icing sugar as soft butter and stir through whatever takes your fancy. Coffee essence, citrus zest or cocoa powder are brilliant options. Use it like glue to stick sponges together, or ice the top of a cake, or pipe it through a nozzle for a decorative finish.

STORAGE
Since you haven't stuffed these sweet treats with loads of preservatives like the shop-bought equivalent, they won't last as long. A major difference between cakes and biscuits is how they deteriorate. Cakes and sponges go stale with age, while biscuits and pastry go soggy. You can keep them for longer by bunging them into an airtight box or tin as soon as they are cool. Besides, once tucked away from sight they might be a bit safer from the greedy mitts of friends and family.

SHINY LOOK
Before baking pastry or bread, brush the top with a little milk or whisked egg. This wash will give the finished product the glossy shine that will make your stuff look pro.

THE SCIENTIFIC BALANCE
The beauty of working with food is that you can throw flavours together, taste it and adjust to excite your own taste buds. That is until you start baking. Bread, pastry and most desserts will only be guaranteed success if you take care in weighing out the items and following the method.

CLASSIC SPONGE MIX

Softened butter (175g)
Caster sugar (175g)
3 eggs
Self-raising flour (175g)
A drop of vanilla extract

PREHEAT the oven to 180°C.
CREAM the butter and sugar in a bowl until you have a smooth paste that is light and aerated.
BEAT in the eggs one at a time, adding a tablespoon of sifted flour with each one and the vanilla extract with the last egg.
SIEVE in the remaining flour and fold through carefully.
SCRAPE the mix into a round non-stick tin or baking tin lined with greaseproof paper, levelling it off.
BAKE in the preheated oven for 15–20 minutes, until it's golden brown on top and springs back when gently touched with your finger.
TURN out on to a wire rack after cooling in the tin for 10 minutes to cool off completely.

MICROWAVEABLE SPONGE MIX

This delight is brilliant because it only takes minutes to cook. Chuck together your cake mix, bung it into a microwave-proof bowl, cover and nuke the hell out of it in the microwave for just long enough to get the custard sorted. It's fantastic baking without the ... baking!

1 x classic sponge mix
1 shot of milk
Zest of ½ a lemon
4 tbsp golden syrup

MAKE the classic mix as before but remember to add the additional milk and zest at the end.
GRAB a big 3 pint bowl and make sure it's microwaveable.
WARM a spoon under hot water and measure out the syrup in the bottom of the bowl.
SCRAPE the cake mixture on top.
COVER the bowl with a microwaveable plate and put the whole thing in the microwave.
NUKE it on full power for 4 minutes then leave it to rest for 2 minutes.
TURN out onto a plate and dig in immediately.

CUPCAKES

1 x classic sponge mix (see page 206)
Milk (160ml)
Icing sugar (300g)
Pink food colouring
A dozen fresh cherries
Cupcake cases

PREHEAT the oven to 180°C.

MAKE the classic sponge mix, then stir the milk in at the end.

DIVIDE the mixture between 12 cupcake cases, filling each half way up.

BAKE for 20 minutes, until risen, golden and a skewer comes out clean.

ALLOW to cool on a wire rack.

SIEVE the icing sugar into a large bowl and add a few drops of pink food colouring along with enough water (1–2 tbsp) to make a smooth, thick paste.

SPOON the icing onto the cakes. Don't worry if it dribbles down the side a little as this all adds to the character.

TOP each cake with a whole cherry and leave to one side for the icing to set.

STORE in an air-tight container for up to 3 days . . . but chances are they'll be scoffed long before that!

COCONUT AND LIME DRIZZLE CAKE

1 × classic sponge mix (see page 206)
Coconut milk (200ml)
Caster sugar (150g)
2 limes

MAKE the sponge as in the classic recipe and bake in a 900g loaf tin for 30 minutes (ensure it's a non-stick tin or line it well with baking paper).
POUR the coconut milk into a small pan with the sugar and bring to a simmer.
DISSOLVE the sugar and simmer for 5 minutes.
ADD the lime zest and juice and reduce further until thick and syrupy.
WHEN the cake is done, pour the lime drizzle mixture over it while still warm and in its tin.
LEAVE to cool completely in the tin before turning out.

UPSIDE-DOWN PEAR CAKE

2 pears
2 tbsp brown sugar
Cider (100ml)
1 × classic sponge mix (see page 206)

PREHEAT the oven to 180°C.
PEEL the pears, core them and cut into quarters.
LAY them in a deep baking tray.
SPRINKLE with brown sugar and splash on the cider.
ROAST in the preheated oven for 15 minutes while you make the sponge mix.
ARRANGE the partly cooked pears in the bottom of a cake tin, getting rid of as much liquid as possible.
SPOON the sponge mix over the pears.
BAKE for 25 minutes, until golden on top and cooked through.
TIP upside-down and serve.

Top Tip
Once the cookie dough has been made, slap it onto a sheet of greaseproof paper and roll it into a large sausage, twisting both ends to seal. Stick in the fridge for up to a week, slice off cookies and bake as and when you want. Just add a minute or two to the cooking time as you'll be cooking them from cold.

COOKIES

Everyone has a favourite cookie … and this way we can all get our own way. Think of it as the pic 'n' mix cookie range. Make individual cookies and personalise them or shape the mix into one giant cookie pizza so everyone can grab a slice!

Softened butter (170g)
White sugar (100g)
Brown sugar (200g)
1 egg
Tsp vanilla extract
Plain flour (250g)
Tsp baking powder
Pinch of salt
Personalised ingredients (see below)

PREHEAT the oven to 170°C.
MEASURE the butter and sugars into a bowl and beat with a spoon for a couple of minutes, until fluffy and light. (Blast in the microwave for a few seconds if the butter is rock hard!)
CRACK in the egg and beat well.
DRIP in the vanilla extract and stir through.
SIEVE in the remaining dry ingredients and fold the cookie dough together until combined.
ADD your personalised extra ingredient – see some variations below for inspiration.
SPOON a teaspoon of the mix onto a non-stick or lined baking tray and gently flatten.
REPEAT until all the dough has been used, keeping a reasonable space between the cookies for them to spread.
BAKE in the preheated oven for 2 minutes. They will still be soft but should be slightly golden around the edges.
LEAVE on the tray for a minute or two before lifting them onto a wire rack to cool completely.
SCOFF them or store in an airtight container for up to 3 days.

Variety of options
100g chopped milk chocolate and 100g chopped hazelnuts
Zest of an orange and 100g dried cranberries
100g chopped glacé cherries and 100g toasted almond flakes
(plus a drop of almond extract)
A handful of chopped stem ginger
A handful of fresh blueberries
100g toasted oats
150g Smarties

CHUNKY CHOCOLATE BROWNIES

It's your mate's birthday and you've forgotten a present. Oh @#%! Well it's the thought that counts, right? So dash into the kitchen and knock up these brownies to save the day. A cheat's version of the kids' fave, it involves no complex baking manoeuvres and the secret ingredient (banana – sshhhhh!) will keep it moist for days. By the time you take it out of the oven they'll be eating out of the palm of your hands.

Dark chocolate (175g)
Butter (175g)
2 ripe bananas
2 eggs
Self-raising flour (120g)
Caster sugar (120g)
Handful of pecans
Icing sugar

PREHEAT the oven to 175°C.

SNAP the chocolate into a plastic bowl and add the butter.

MELT in the microwave – TAKE CARE not to overheat it or it'll split (see Top Tip).

PEEL and mash the bananas into a large mixing bowl, then beat in the eggs.

SIEVE the flour into the eggy mix and add the sugar and a pinch of salt.

SPILL the chocolatey butter into the mixture and combine.

LOB in the pecan nuts, mix and pop it all into a greased rectangular pan.

BAKE on the middle shelf of the oven for 30 minutes.

LET it cool for 30 minutes to firm up.

TURN out, dust with icing sugar, cut and serve.

Top Tip
Be careful – you can make or break this dish during the melting process. Remove the chocolate from the microwave before it's completely melted. The residual heat will finish the job

BLUEBERRY FLAPJACKS

These blueberry flapjacks (bargain-bucket items for less than 40p a slice) will keep for days and are considered by us a gold-dust commodity when you need a pick-me-up. However, a word of advice: stash them away out of sight, otherwise your family, flatmates or colleagues will snap 'em up without a second thought!

Butter (170g)
4 tbsp brown sugar
Golden syrup (200g)
Tsp ground cinnamon
Rolled oats or porridge oats (300g)
Fresh blueberries (150g)

PREHEAT oven to 180°C.
MELT the butter, sugar, syrup and cinnamon in a saucepan.
BUBBLE for a minute before removing from heat.
FOLD in the oats until fully combined.
SCATTER the blueberries into the mix and carefully stir through.
TIP into a lined, deep baking tray.
BAKE for 20–25 minutes until golden.
COOL in the tin, cutting into portions before it's completely cold.

MACARONS

A dainty sweet treat that you can make dozens of and share at any special occasion. These beautiful French patisseries were requested by dozens of our YouTube subscribers, including none other than the comedy blogger Jenna Marbles, and so we knew we had to get them SORTED. Our version is made easier by skipping the traditional and slightly tricky boiling-sugar stage, yet still makes light macarons of all colours that can be sandwiched with any sticky filling of your choice. You will need three piping bags or, if you don't have any, a sandwich bag with the corner snipped off can work just as well.

3 egg whites
Caster sugar (75g)
Ground almonds (125g)
Icing sugar (175g)
Flavourings (raspberry, lemon, vanilla)
Food colourings (pink, yellow, blue)
Fillings (raspberry jam, lemon curd, Nutella)

sortedfood.com/
macarons

SEPARATE the egg whites from the yolks and in a clean, dry bowl, whisk the whites until thick and glossy.
ADD the caster sugar and whisk again until stiff.
SIEVE the almonds and icing sugar into the bowl and carefully fold in, retaining as much air as possible.
DIVIDE the mixture between three bowls and add a few drops of the following colourings and flavourings to each:
– raspberry flavour and pink colouring
– lemon flavour and yellow colouring
– vanilla flavour and blue colouring.
PUT each one into a separate piping bag.
LINE a baking tray with baking paper or a silicon mat and pipe small circles (3cm across) onto the tray, leaving a small gap between each macaron. You need to do even numbers of each colour, because they're going to be sandwiched together after they're cooked.
PUT the tray to one side for 15 minutes to allow a slight skin to form.
PREHEAT the oven to 160°C.
PICK the tray up and drop it onto a flat surface from a small height . . . this forms the 'feet' that are associated with macarons.
BAKE for 15 minutes, then remove and allow to cool at room temperature until completely cold.
SANDWICH the macarons with the different fillings: raspberry jam for the pink, lemon curd for the yellow and Nutella for the blue.
EAT within 24 hours, as they go stale very quickly.

PUDDINGS

This chapter surely contains the best bits – the nuts! The dogs! The cherry on top!

It doesn't matter how strong-willed you are and how menacingly that calorie counter haunts you – every once in a while, for one night only, you just have to go the full monty. These are serious crowd-pleasers to punctuate the end of a wicked meal, leaving your friends and family happier than ever. Go on – make 'em weak at the knees!

Most of these pleasure-seeking desserts can be made ahead of time when the kitchen is calm and you can put all your love and attention into crafting them, making any cock-ups on the quiet! The secret is to keep it simple but then do the flamboyant presentation bit to give it the wow factor.

And besides, the proof of the pudding is in the eating, so we guess it would be rude not to, wouldn't it?

And remember, keep an eye on our website at www.sortedfood.com for more great recipes.

ICE CREAM

BASIC MIX

Double cream (600ml)
Condensed milk (397g)
Vanilla pod or ½ tsp vanilla extract

WHIP the cream lightly until it forms soft peaks.
STIR through the condensed milk and vanilla along with your flavour of choice – some ideas are below.
POUR into a suitable container and freeze for a couple of hours.
WHISK the mix up now that it is a bit slushy then return to the freezer to solidify completely.
LEAVE the ice cream out of the freezer to soften for 10 minutes before serving.
ENJOY pure perfection!

CHOCOLATE COOKIE

Dark chocolate (200g), melted
Crushed chocolate cookies (200g)

BANANA AND PEANUT

2 tbsp crunchy peanut butter
1 banana, mashed

BROWN BREAD

Yes... that's brown bread!

2 slices brown bread, toasted and crumbed
Sprinkle of mixed spice

BERRY AND ALMOND

Plenty of crushed berries
Handful of toasted almonds

CRUMBLE

OK, so we have a confession. Throughout the book we've been subtly trying to transform you from complete kitchen novices into culinary geniuses by introducing no-brainer nosh that would put your mum's cooking to shame. And these ones just might tip the scales. Our versions of the classic crumble are rigged with stunning combinations of fruit designed to implode in your mouth, all topped off with a devastatingly delicious variety of crumbles. An effortless dessert, and one that will definitely impress.

TRADITIONAL APPLE AND CINNAMON CRUMBLE

Cooking apples (about 1 kg)
Double shot of orange juice
Brown sugar (120g)
Sprinkle of cinnamon
Plain flour (120g)
Cold butter (80g)

PREHEAT the oven to 180°C.
CORE the apples, then peel and cut into chunks.
PLACE them in a pan with the orange juice, a handful of the sugar and the cinnamon.
STEW the fruit for just a few minutes, until the apple chunks begin to soften around the edges.
TIP into an ovenproof dish.
SIFT the flour into a clean bowl and add the diced butter.
RUB the two together with your fingertips until it all looks like breadcrumbs.
STIR through the rest of the sugar and sprinkle over the half-cooked apples.
BAKE for about 30 minutes, until golden on top and the apples are beginning to bubble up at the sides.

HOMEMADE CUSTARD

½ a vanilla pod or ½ tsp vanilla extract
Milk (500ml)
6 egg yolks
2 heaped tbsp caster sugar

SCRAPE seeds from the pod and add them (or the extract) to the milk in a pan.
BRING to a gentle boil, stirring occasionally.
WHISK the egg yolks and sugar in a clean bowl.
POUR the boiling milk over the egg yolks while whisking.
RETURN to the pan and stir continuously over a very gentle heat until the custard thickens and will coat the back of a spoon. Take care, 'cos if you heat it too quickly or for too long you'll end up with sweet scrambled egg – not a good look!
TAKE off the heat and pass through a sieve to remove any lumps.
CHILL and serve cold, or re-heat as required in the microwave.

RHUBARB AND GINGER WITH GRANOLA CRUMBLE

Wow your guests with this easy twist on a crumble-style dessert. This will make six individual puds in those posh presentation rings (or use immaculately clean tins with top and bottom removed).

Rhubarb (1kg)
Caster sugar (200g)
1 orange
Preserved stem ginger (30g)
A bowl of luxury granola cereal

WASH the rhubarb and cut into chunks the size of your thumb.
STICK them in a pan with the sugar and a few drops of water, and cook over a gentle heat for about 10 minutes.
ZEST the orange and finely dice the stem ginger, then add them to the partially stewed fruit.
LAY the granola on a baking tray and warm through in the oven.
ASSEMBLE the crumbles on individual plates by stacking the cooked rhubarb in the rings and topping with the warm and crisp granola then gently lift the rings away.
SERVE with ice cream.

PLUM AND VANILLA WITH FLAPJACK CRUMBLE

Plums (about 12)
Brown sugar (120g)
Vanilla pod
Butter (100g)
Golden syrup (125g)
Porridge oats (250g)

PREHEAT the oven to 180°C.
STONE and quarter the plums and stick them in a pan with a handful of the sugar and the split vanilla pod.
SPLASH in a shot or two of water and cook for 3–4 minutes over a gentle heat until the fruit starts to soften.
DUMP the partly stewed fruit into an ovenproof dish.
MELT the butter, syrup and remaining sugar in a pan until the sugar has dissolved.
STIR through the porridge oats, then spread over the plums.
BAKE in the preheated oven for 25 minutes, until golden and gooey.
LEAVE to stand for 10 minutes before serving a whopping great portion with ice cream.

APRICOT AND GINGER GRATIN

This dessert was one of those 'eureka!' moments whilst on a trip to Falmouth a few years back. Towards the end of a busy day of filming, we still needed a sweet dessert ... the problem was we had no food left! Cue frantic suggestions of random food groups that might just go together, and scavenging around empty cupboards like rabid dogs on heat.

The result? A (just in-date) tin of apricots, the remains of some cream cheese and a half-eaten packet of ginger nut biscuits. It wasn't looking promising, but Ben being Ben pulled it out of the bag and came up with this little beauty!

After some refining once we got back home, this turned into something fantastically impressive ... a classic family crumble served as a fancy dessert.

Apricot halves in syrup (400g)
Cream cheese (200g)
2 tbsp icing sugar
Dash of vanilla extract
Couple of sprigs of fresh mint, chopped
Ginger nut biscuits (150g)

PREHEAT the oven to 180°C.
DRAIN the apricots and arrange cut-side up on a shallow baking dish.
BEAT together the cream cheese, sugar, vanilla and mint.
SPOON a dollop of cheese mix onto each apricot half.
PUT the biscuits into a freezer bag, cover with a tea towel, bash to a coarse crumb and sprinkle over the cream cheese.
BAKE for 5–10 minutes until the cheese begins to ooze.

SWEET PASTRY CASE

Plain flour (250g)
Pinch of salt
Cold butter (125g)
Icing sugar (50g)
2 eggs
Shot of milk if required

THE DOUGH
SIEVE the flour and salt into a bowl.
CUT the butter into cubes and rub into the flour with your fingertips, until the mixture resembles breadcrumbs.
FOLD through the sugar, then add the beaten eggs.
BIND into a dough, then tip out onto a flour or sugar-dusted worktop and knead very lightly for a second or two to remove any cracks.
ADD a splash of milk if the dough is still cracking, but be careful not to overwork it!
WRAP the dough in cling film and chill in the fridge for an hour before using. (It can stay in the fridge like this for up to a week if necessary.)

LINING A PIE OR TART TIN
ROLL out the chilled dough with a rolling pin on a cold, floured and flat surface until it is the thickness of a pound coin and 5cm larger than your tin to allow for shrinkage.
TRANSFER the pastry by rolling it gently around the rolling pin.
UNROLL it over the tin, ensuring that the pastry overhangs the edges by at least 5cm.
LIFT the overhanging dough with one hand while pressing carefully into the base and sides of the tin. Do not stretch the pastry or force it at this stage. Leave the overhang on the pastry.
CHILL in the fridge for 15 minutes.

BAKING BLIND
PREHEAT the oven to 200°C.
PRICK the base of the pastry tart with a fork and cover with a round of greaseproof paper.
FILL with baking beans, dried lentils or rice. These act as a weight to stop the pastry rising.
BAKE for 15 minutes in the preheated oven, then remove the greaseproof paper and beans and bake for a further 5–10 minutes.
CUT away the pastry overhang with a sharp knife when cool, leaving a perfectly smooth and level finish to your tart case.

FRESH FRUITY TART

Double cream (200ml)
½ a vanilla pod or tsp vanilla extract
1 x homemade custard (see page 229)
1 x sweet pastry case
Selection of colourful fruit
(strawberries, kiwis, peaches, purple grapes, mandarin segments)
2 tbsp apricot jam
Icing sugar

sortedfood.com/
fruitcustardtart

WHIP the cream until you have soft peaks.

SCRAPE out the seeds from the vanilla pod or add the vanilla extract and fold into the cream with the custard.

SPOON the creamy vanilla custard into the pastry case.

PREPARE all the fruit as neatly as possible and arrange in the pastry case in rows or sections of colour.

MELT the jam in a bowl in the microwave, then brush it over the finished tart to give it a shine.

DUST with icing sugar and serve – always best eaten at room temperature.

BANOFFEE PIE

Tin of condensed milk (397g)
4 × small individual sweet pastry cases (see recipe on page 234)
Double cream (200ml)
Handful of chopped hazelnuts
3–4 bananas
Few squares of dark chocolate

PLACE the unopened tin of condensed milk in a saucepan and add water to come halfway up the side of the tin.
BRING to the boil and simmer for 2½ hours. Keep topping up the pan with water so that it doesn't boil dry.
LEAVE the tin to cool completely. (Why not make several of these at a time? They keep for months if not opened.)
OPEN the tin to reveal glossy toffee and half-fill your pastry cases with it.
WHIP the cream until soft peaks form and spread over the toffee.
TOAST the hazelnuts in a dry pan until they go golden.
PEEL and slice the bananas and arrange them generously on top just before serving.
DECORATE by grating over some dark chocolate and a sprinkle of the toasted nuts.

CHOCOLATE AND AMARETTI TART

Plain chocolate (100g)
Softened butter (125g)
Caster sugar (125g)
3 large eggs
Self-raising flour (25g)
Ground almonds (125g)
Amaretti biscuits (50g)
1 × sweet pastry case (200g)
Tin of pitted cherries (400g)
Handful of flaked almonds

PREHEAT the oven to 150°C.
BREAK UP the chocolate and melt in the microwave (see page 216) or in a small heatproof bowl over a pan of barely simmering water.
BEAT the butter and sugar in a large bowl until creamy and light.
STIR in the eggs one at a time until smooth.
FOLD in the flour and ground almonds.
CRUSH the amaretti biscuits and carefully add these to the mix with the melted chocolate.
SPOON half of the mix into the tart case.
SCATTER over a handful of the drained cherries and cover with the remainder of the mix.
SPRINKLE with the almond flakes and bake for 1 hour.
COOL in the tin for 15 minutes before attempting to remove.

MERINGUE

PAVLOVA

ROULADE

MERINGUE MIX

4 egg whites
Caster sugar (120g)
Icing sugar (120g)

SEPARATE the egg whites from their yolks and put the whites into a clean bowl.
WHISK them up to stiff peaks.
MEASURE in the caster sugar and whisk until you reach stiff peaks again.
SIFT in the icing sugar and carefully fold together.

PAVLOVA

1 × meringue mix
Double cream (250ml)
2 tbsp icing sugar
½ tsp vanilla extract
Plenty of your favourite vibrant fresh fruit

PREHEAT the oven to 125°C.
SPOON the meringue mixture into a piping bag or a clean sandwich bag with the corner snipped off.
SQUEEZE it through a star nozzle onto a baking tray lined with baking paper to form little individual nests.
BAKE for 1½ hours with a tea towel wedged in the oven door to keep it slightly open and let out any steam. The nests should be dry enough to pick up but still have a slightly chewy centre.
WHIP up the double cream to stiff peaks and fold in the icing sugar and vanilla.
DOLLOP it onto the cooled nests and pile on as much neatly prepared fruit as you dare.

ROULADE

1 × meringue mix
Double cream (250ml)
2 tbsp icing sugar
½ tsp vanilla extract
Plenty of your favourite, vibrant fresh fruit
Cocoa powder
Nuts, chopped and toasted

PREHEAT the oven to 150°C.
SPREAD the meringue mix in a thin layer right across a lined baking tray.
BAKE for 30–35 minutes until crisp on the outside but chewy in the centre. Allow to fully cool, then place the meringue still on its baking paper on a clean tea towel, making it easier to roll.
WHIP up the double cream to stiff peaks, fold in the sifted sugar and vanilla and spread a thin layer over the whole sheet of meringue.
SCATTER a variety of fruit over the cream and carefully roll the meringue to make the classic roulade.
DECORATE with a dusting of cocoa powder and a few toasted nuts.

BASIC CHOCOLATE MOUSSE

You may be put off making puddings as you think you haven't got the time or the money. Well, we intend to put an end to this malicious rumour right now, so chuck your shoddy excuses down the drain and start by whipping up these little beauties. They're cheap, tasty and quick to prepare. Then bung 'em in the fridge and serve as and when. You'll be able to sit down and enjoy dinner with friends without the cold sweat dripping down your back as you panic about dessert. Oh, and did we say they look pretty damn cool too.

Dark, milk or white chocolate (250g)
Milk (100ml)
Double cream (280ml)
3 large egg whites

CRACK the chocolate into small pieces and place in a heatproof bowl with the milk.
HEAT in the microwave (see page 216) or over a pan of gently simmering water until melted and silky smooth.
ADD any additional flavourings (see below).
LEAVE to cool for 10 minutes.
WHIP the cream to soft but floppy peaks.
WHISK the egg whites in another bowl to soft peaks.
FOLD the cream into the chocolate mixture as carefully as possible, then do the same with the egg whites.
DIVIDE into individual glasses, dishes or cups and chill for at least 4 hours.

CHOCOLATE ORANGE MOUSSE

1 × basic chocolate mousse (using milk chocolate)
Grated zest of 1 large orange

WHITE CHOCOLATE AND RASPBERRY MOUSSE

1 × basic chocolate mousse (using white chocolate)
Small punnet of fresh raspberries, half of them mashed up

CAPPUCCINO MOUSSE

1 × basic chocolate mousse (using dark chocolate)
3 tsp 'Camp chicory and coffee essence' or
2 tbsp strong black espresso coffee

BUNCH OF FOOLS

You'd be one not to give this simple and tasty pud a go. Fools can look so pro if you take care to layer them up as you go along, but they taste just as good if slopped in a bowl and devoured as a comforting pud on a well-deserved lazy night in. A DVD marathon and a bowl of Ben and Jamie's fruit fool would fit the bill perfectly – a gloriously satisfying substitute for a tub of your favourite American ice cream, and far less likely to put pressure on your arteries or your bank balance.

CLASSIC FOOL MIX

Crème fraîche (150ml)
Natural yoghurt (150ml)
2 tbsp icing sugar
Additional ingredients (see below and pages 246 and 249)

BEAT the crème fraîche and yoghurt together in a large bowl.
SIFT in the icing sugar.
PREPARE all the additional ingredients as required (see below).
LAYER into a big bowl or fancy glasses and garnish accordingly.

BANANA AND HONEY

Handful of flaked almonds
1 banana
Squeeze of runny honey
1 x classic fool mix

TOAST the almonds in a dry pan until they begin to colour and smell like popcorn.
PEEL and thinly slice the banana.
CONSTRUCT the dessert by squeezing in layers of honey, banana, classic fool mix and cooled almond flakes.

ETON MESS

1 x meringue mix (see page 241)
Handful of mixed soft red berries
1 x classic fool mix (see page 245)

MAKE a sheet of meringue as for the roulade on page 241 and then break up into small pieces.

MASH half of the berries and leave the rest whole.

CONSTRUCT the dessert by combining mashed berries, meringue and classic fool mix to gain a marbled effect.

FINISH with meringue pieces and whole berries.

LEMON AND BLACKCURRANT FOOL

¼ of a packet of HobNob biscuits (75g)
1 x classic fool mix (see page 245)
Lemon curd (100g)
Tin of blackberries in syrup (400g)

CRUMBLE up the biscuits into small chunks and stir through the classic fool mix (leaving some aside to garnish the top with later).
DRAIN the blackberries and fold half of them through the mix with the lemon curd to create a marbled effect.
LAYER into serving glasses with the rest of the berries.
FINISH with more HobNob pieces.

CAKE IN A MUG

This perfect little individual cake was our first video recipe to go viral. Capturing everything that SORTED stands for, this is quick, simple food at its best. So if the thought of baking a chocolate pudding conjures up images of effort, time and mess, yet you still want to treat yourself, then this no-bake option is ready in minutes and perfect to snuggle up with in front of the TV.

2 tbsp self-raising flour (not heaped or level but in between)
2 tbsp caster sugar
1 tbsp cocoa
1 tsp instant coffee powder
1 small egg
1 tbsp milk
1 tbsp sunflower oil
A few chocolate buttons

sortedfood.com/
cakeinamug

GRAB a large mug.
SPOON dry ingredients into the mug and mix well.
CRACK in the egg and whisk with a fork to combine.
DRIZZLE in the milk and oil and stir.
DROP in a few chocolate buttons.
COOK in a microwave for 2½ minutes on full power.
LEAVE to rest for 1 minute then eat sprinkled with icing sugar, or with lashings of cream or ice cream.

Now ... to wash all this grub down we need a little something to wet our whistle. Help is on hand from our resident drink doctor as we prescribe a dose of wet and wonderful ideas to quench your thirst.

Our smoothies will get those early mornings off to an energetic and fruity start, or if you'd rather chill out in the summer months try our refreshing, homemade milkshakes or fruit punches.

At SORTED we rarely need an excuse for a party ... so here's to testing out a few new speciality punches and 'mocktails' with enough style and flair to become the talking point of any night in with your mates.

As ever, these ideas and flavours are only the beginning of what's possible. Why not slip into mixologist mode and see what you can come up with.

Cheers!

DRINKS

THE FIRST MEETING OF
SORTED WAY BACK IN 2008.
WHERE IT ALL BEGAN

SHAKES AND SMOOTHIES

Milkshakes – a little bit naughty but definitely nice! We could try to convince you that they're a fantastic way to boost your calcium levels and provide you with the necessary dose of vitamin X, but to be frank it's all a load of tosh. And who cares? They taste superb!

BASIC SHAKE

Cup of milk
2 scoops of ice cream
Your additional flavouring (see below)

SLOSH the milk into a blender with your chosen ice cream.
TIP in your additional flavour, breaking things up a little if they're large.
WHIZZ for about 30 seconds – long enough to blend in the chunky bits but not so long that you begin to lose the thick and creamy consistency.
POUR into a tall glass and garnish with an array of fruit, chocolate shavings, marshmallows or a dusting of cocoa powder.
DIVE straight in and enjoy.

Add some flavour:
Honey crunch – vanilla ice cream and a packet of Maltesers.

After-dinner delight – mint choc chip ice cream and a handful of crisp after-dinner mints.

Wimbledon Common – strawberry ice cream and a few jammy dodgers, topped off with mini marshmallows.

FROZEN SMOOTHIE TIME

Smoothies have taken the world by storm, competing with designer drinks such as the mochaccino or skinny soya latte. But while some smoothies are dairy-based, we prefer to keep the cows at bay and stick to purely fruity options. Here are some of our favourites, so have a go at these and then experiment with some of your own ideas. Get blitzing!

Apple juice (250ml)
Your fruit of choice (150g):
1 Strawberry and banana
2 Pineapple and mango
3 Melon and mandarin
4 Apple, pear, blueberry and blackberry

WASH or peel your chosen fruits.
CHOP them up into small regular-shaped pieces, ideally the size of a raspberry.
LAY them out on a tray and freeze. If you've got more than you need and you want to be organised, store 150g batches in the freezer until needed.
POUR the apple juice into a blender and tip in 150g of the frozen fruit that takes your fancy.
BLITZ for 30 seconds, until your ice-cold fruit smoothie is lump-free and thick.
EMPTY into a glass and slurp through a straw.

Top Tip
You can also buy frozen fruit pre-prepared at some supermarkets. Just add fruit juice, blitz it and Bob's your uncle.

MOCKTAILS

A traditional mojito will bring a touch of Cuban sunshine to any bar and these two great alcohol-free **SORTED** variations never disappoint. They're a perfect balance of sweet cane sugar, bitter lime and refreshing mint, muddled with bucket-loads of ice.

ELDERFLOWER MOJITO

2 brown sugar cubes
½ a lime, cut into wedges
5 mint leaves
Plenty of ice
Elderflower cordial (50ml)
Apple juice (50ml)

PASSION FRUIT MOJITO

2 brown sugar cubes
½ a lime, cut into wedges
5 mint leaves
Plenty of ice
Passion fruit juice (100ml)

STICK the sugar cubes, lime wedges and mint into a tall glass and bash them up with a muddle stick or the end of a wooden spoon.
CRUSH some ice in a blender or in a clean tea towel with a rolling pin.
DUMP a handful into the glass to half fill it.
POUR in the cordial and/or juice and stir the drink well.
SERVE with fresh lime, a sprig of mint and a straw or two.

ZOMBIE

For a silky touch of class with your drinks why not give this one a go? The egg white transforms a regular fruit punch into something that really deserves top slot on any cocktail menu.

½ a lime, cut into wedges
½ a shot of grenadine (12.5ml)
2 shots of pineapple juice (50ml)
2 shots of orange juice (50ml)
½ an egg white (10ml)
Ice

MEASURE all of the ingredients into a cocktail shaker.
ADD a few cubes of ice.
SECURE the lid and shake well until a frothy and silky liquid forms.
POUR into a glass over more ice.

Top Tip
As with most cocktails, it's all about the razzle-dazzle presentation. To really get the wow factor why not go to the effort of hollowing out a pinapple? Slice off the top and scoop out the flesh, taking care not to pierce the watertight skin. This is nature's answer to a fancy cocktail glass and raises eyebrows at every occasion. It can be washed out when finished and re-used all night long.

PUNCH PARTY

For the moments when making one drink at a time just won't do the job, simply whip out a punch. (This might sound like a wild act of violence but it stems from the word 'puncheon', the 72-gallon cask in which they used to mix it – but unless you want to bath in it, we're guessing you won't need quite that much!)

These are the new pre-going-out beverages, some seriously sophisticated concoctions that thrust a little Sex and the City glamour back into our lives. Whether you're sipping this with the girls or 'manning up' with the lads, mooch around and get people to chip in for the alcohol, throw them together and enjoy whilst playing every drinking game under the sun. Tasty, sweet and best of all, idiot-proof.

GRAB the largest bowl you can find.
POUR in the ingredients and juices you love best (see below).
BALANCE the sweet and sour to your own taste by adding some sugar syrup and/or lime juice.
STIR well and ladle into glasses over ice.

POMMIE APPLE

Equal quantities of apple juice and pomegranate juice
Twice as much lemonade
A good glug of gin

GINGER FIZZ

Equal quantities of blueberry juice and cranberry juice
Half as much ginger ale
Several shots of vodka

SUNNY PASSION

Equal quantities of :
Orange juice
Grapefruit juice
Pineapple juice
Passionfruit juice
Plenty of coconut rum

CITRUS COCKTAIL

Believe it or not, this was where the SORTED videos all started. While away with the lads writing and testing recipes for our first book, we got the urge, spurred on by alcohol, to dance ... looking back, we question how normal this is! The 1988 movie Cocktail, which catapulted Tom Cruise's smooth bartending skills onto the big screen, merged with Morecambe and Wise's infamous breakfast scene as we dazzled even ourselves with this simply amazing cocktail. Remember that this is as fun to make as it is to swig.

1 lime
1 lemon
1 orange
Tin of pineapple in syrup (230g)
Orange juice (200ml)
Handful of ice cubes
Healthy splash of vodka

sortedfood.com/
citruscocktail

HALVE the citrus fruits and squeeze into a blender (try to avoid pips).
ADD the pineapple.
CRUSH the ice and add to the mix with the orange juice.
SPLASH in a 'responsible' measure of vodka.
BLITZ to a slushy texture.
POUR into a glass and finish with lime zest.

TRICKY'S FRUIT PUNCH

Vodka (1L)
Malibu/coconut-flavoured rum (1L)
Orange juice (3L)
Cranberry juice (2L)

SWIRL the alcohol into the bottom of a big bowl.
POUR in the fruit juices and stir well.
DUMP in the middle of the table and ladle into glasses.

CHOCOLATE HOTTIE

**This needs no introduction ... we all know and love a good
hot chocolate and this is one of the best!**

6 tsp sugar
6 tsp cocoa powder
Cup of milk (300ml)
Cup of single cream (300ml)
Pinch of cinnamon
½ tsp vanilla extract
Whipped cream

PUT the sugar, cocoa and milk in a saucepan and heat until
all is dissolved.
ADD the cream, cinnamon and vanilla.
HEAT until almost boiling.
MIX well and serve, topped with whipped cream.

MEALS TO IMPRESS

Meal 1 Warming Food for Friends
Spicy red pepper soup
Lamb with ratatouille
Cheeky chocolate cherry pots

Meal 2 A Perfect Summer Date
Warm asparagus and
beetroot salad
Chilli garlic prawns on
a lemon saffron risotto
Sublime strawberry 'Champagne' jelly

Meal 3 Veggie Meal to Impress
Red onion tartlet with
creamy goat's cheese
Gorgonzola gnocchi with spinach
and toasted walnuts
Baileys soufflé-style ice cream

Meal 4 Family Sunday Lunch
Stuffed mushrooms
Deconstructed Chicken Kiev
Iced lemon and ginger tortes

Finding yourself a boyfriend or girlfriend doesn't come cheap and eating out together can also eat away at your bank balance. During the sickeningly cringey 'honeymoon' period money slips through your fingers. Before you know it, the floating halo above your other half's head disappears and reality hits you where it hurts. All that wining and dining, supposed one-off treats and silly childish gifts mount up, and your bank manager is having a right fit. You need to somehow bring the spark back into your relationship without filing for bankruptcy. And, no, selling your body on the streets isn't an option.

We proudly present you with the solution— delicious and dead-easy meal plans that will soon have you right back in the apple-of-your-eye's good books. Picture the scene: you're enjoying a classy three-course delight at a posh restaurant, surrounded by a blaze of scented candles and listening to Barry White. Alternatively, you're enjoying this posh (but cheap) nosh at your place and not a takeaway leaflet in sight! Who said romance was dead?

WARNING!
Chilli powder can be the work of the devil in the wrong hands. A powerful spice, it can ruin a romantic night if meandering mitts meet sensitive parts of the body. Don't be a mug – remember to wash your hands.

MEAL 1
WARMING FOOD FOR FRIENDS
SERVES 4

One for the cold winter months. What you need at this time is comfort food that will melt your hot date into submission and this meal is the key to securing that all-important clincher. We've designed a three-course extravaganza that will knock the socks off anyone you set out to impress. Allow us to introduce our opening act of spicy wholesome soup, followed by a headliner of posh meat and two veg, succeeded by a firework finale that we call cheeky chocolate cherry pots.

STARTER
SPICY RED PEPPER SOUP

1 large onion
Shot of olive oil
3 red peppers
1 large potato
Veg stock (750ml)
½ tsp paprika
¼ tsp chilli powder
Dollop of natural yoghurt
Handful of freshly chopped chives

PEEL and slice the onion and fry gently in the olive oil in a deep pan for 5–10 minutes.
DE-SEED and roughly chop the peppers, peel and grate the potato and then add both to the cooked onions.
DISSOLVE a stock cube in 750ml of boiling water, add the stock to the pan and sprinkle in the spices.
SIMMER for half an hour.
BLITZ to a smooth soup, return to the pan, reheat and season.
WHISK in the yoghurt, having removed the pan from the heat, and stir through the chopped chives. Serve with some crusty rustic bread.

DID YOU KNOW?
The active ingredient in chilli peppers is a compound called capsaicin, which gives it that unique sting. Capsaicin triggers the release of endorphins in the brain, which has a pain-relieving effect similar to that of morphine.

MAIN COURSE
LAMB WITH RATATOUILLE

8 medium tomatoes
1 red onion
2 red peppers
1 aubergine
3 courgettes
2 cloves of garlic
Olive oil
Sprinkle of fresh mint

Tbsp fennel seeds
2 tbsp flour
Lamb neck fillet (600g)
Olive oil

6 wholemeal pitta breads
Handful of feta cheese

PREHEAT the oven to 200°C.
DICE the tomatoes, onion, peppers, aubergine and courgettes into
2.5cm cubes. Peel and crush the garlic.
TRANSFER to a large baking tray.
DRIZZLE over olive oil and season generously with salt and
black pepper.
ROAST for 40 minutes, tossing occasionally.
MIX the fennel seeds and flour together on a board.
ROLL the lamb over the flour/fennel seed mix until you achieve an
even coating.
HEAT a generous shot of olive oil in a frying pan and fry the lamb
until golden on all sides. Slide it into the oven for 5 minutes (rare),
8 minutes (medium) or 12 minutes (well done).
REST the meat for a couple of minutes before slicing.
STIR the mint through the ratatouille.
SLIP the pitta breads into a toaster till crisp, then slice into strips.
SPOON the ratatouille onto a plate and crumble over the feta cheese.
LAY the lamb on top with pitta on the side.

DESSERT
CHEEKY CHOCOLATE CHERRY POTS

Butter (100g plus extra for greasing)
4 tbsp pitted morello cherries (in syrup)
Plain chocolate (100g)
1 large egg
Brown sugar (100g)
4 tbsp self-raising flour
Cream to serve

PREHEAT the oven to 220°C.
GREASE 4 ramekins with butter and drop a layer of drained cherries into the base of each.
SNAP the chocolate into cubes and put with the 100g of butter, diced, in a plastic bowl.
MELT over a pan of simmering water or, even easier, in the microwave (see page 216).
WHISK the egg and sugar in another bowl until light and fluffy (about 2 minutes).
POUR in the cooled melted chocolate mix and beat again to combine.
SIEVE in the flour and fold carefully until smooth.
SHARE between the ramekins, then bake for 20–25 minutes until risen and just cracking on top.
INVERT puddings onto a plate and carefully shake them out.
DRIZZLE with cream and serve.

NOTE!
Although spongy on the outside these puds should still be gooey in the centre – very rich and dangerously sensuous. Chocolate contains methylxanthines which apparently work wonders for stimulating conduction and transmission of nerve impulses, helping to heighten sensitivity.

MEAL 2
PERFECT SUMMER DATE
SERVES 2

When you have someone special round to your place the last thing you want to do is bloat the hell out of 'em by stuffing them with enough food to feed a baby elephant. Consequently, a bout of flatulence and tiredness follows, which ain't good for anyone. This summery three-course menu is as light as a Quaver, with a hassle-free starter, a tangy risotto for main and a sublime jelly to finish. This menu is so sexy, seductive and cool we guarantee your partner will be putty in your hands by the final mouthful.

STARTER
WARM ASPARAGUS AND BEETROOT SALAD

Bunch of asparagus spears (250g)
2 shots of olive oil
Small pack of cooked beetroot, not in vinegar (250g)
Dollop of horseradish sauce
Dash of white wine vinegar
Parmesan
Handful of fresh parsley
Couple of spring onions

sortedfood.com/
asparagusandbeetroot

PREHEAT the oven to 200°C.
TRIM the stalky base from asparagus spears and wash.
PLACE on a baking tray, toss in a shot of oil and season with salt and pepper.
ROAST for 6–8 minutes until slightly soft to touch.
CHOP the beetroot into bite-sized pieces and add to the almost-cooked asparagus to heat through.
WHISK the remaining oil, horseradish sauce and vinegar together to create a dressing. Season.
ARRANGE the asparagus and beetroot on a plate so they overlap.
SPRINKLE over Parmesan shavings, garnish with parsley and finely sliced spring onions, then drizzle with the dressing.
ENJOY as a perfectly delicate start to any romantic meal.

NOTE!
Asparagus contains vitamin A and phosphorus and boosts androsterone levels, an odourless hormone released by men. This, along with their suggestive shape, can really heat up any sensuous situation.

MAIN
CHILLI GARLIC PRAWNS ON A LEMON SAFFRON RISOTTO

Raw prawns, peeled (250g)
4 tbsp sweet chilli sauce
3 cloves of garlic
Veg stock (1 litre)
Pinch of saffron
Bunch of spring onions
Tsp grated fresh ginger
Knob of butter
Risotto rice (250g)
1 lemon
Drizzle of double cream
Handful of fresh parsley

MARINATE the prawns in the chilli sauce with one peeled and crushed clove of garlic.

MAKE up the vegetable stock with boiled water, or bring your homemade stock to a simmer, and add the saffron to infuse.

SLICE the spring onions and peel and chop the remaining garlic.

SWEAT the onions, ginger and garlic in a deep pan with the butter for a few moments.

STIR in the rice to coat all the grains in butter.

ADD the zest of the lemon and a ladle of stock, stirring continuously.

ADD more stock as the previous ladle is absorbed.

WHEN the rice is plump and cooked (about 20 minutes) heat a dry frying pan, add the prawns and marinade, and sizzle until the prawns turn pink all over.

DRIZZLE the cream into the risotto and finish with chopped parsley and the juice of the lemon.

SEASON, then spoon the risotto onto plates and top with the prawns.

DESSERT
SUBLIME STRAWBERRY
'CHAMPAGNE' JELLY

½ bottle rosé cava (375ml)
Caster sugar (175g)
Gelatin (10g of powder or 4 leaves)
Few sprigs of fresh mint
Handful of fresh strawberries
Double cream, whipped

POP the cava's cork and glug a quarter of the bottle into a pan.
SPOON in the sugar and bring to the boil; simmer until the sugar has dissolved.
SOAK the gelatin (if using leaves) in cold water, squeeze dry and whisk into the hot 'champagne' (or add the powder).
COOL the mixture by sitting the pan in cold water.
TRICKLE another quarter of the bottle of cava into the mix, trying to maintain as much fizz as possible.
STIR through the very finely shredded mint leaves.
SHARE the mixture between 2 glasses.
SUBMERGE the sliced strawberries in the jelly and leave in the fridge to set.
ENJOY with whipped cream!

NOTE!
If you have time you can layer the jelly by filling the glasses up only a third at a time and setting in the fridge. Each time the fruit will remain in suspension rather than floating to the top. The jelly you're not setting will remain liquid if kept in a warm room.

MEAL 3
VEGGIE MEAL TO IMPRESS
SERVES 2

Perhaps it's a meat-free option you and your better half are seeking. In which case this delicately balanced onion and goat's cheese tartlet teases your palette before a plate of feisty Italian dumplings obliterates that insatiable appetite, all topped off with a ridiculously tasty Baileys soufflé-style ice cream. Temptation, fulfilment, pleasure...

STARTER
RED ONION TARTLET WITH
CREAMY GOAT'S CHEESE

1 red onion
Shot of olive oil
Tbsp balsamic vinegar
Tbsp brown sugar
Sheet of ready-rolled puff pastry (125g)
Goat's cheese (75g)
A few cherry tomatoes
Bunch of fresh basil
Handful of crisp salad leaves
Drizzle of salad dressing
Couple of pitted black olives

PREHEAT the oven to 200°C.
PEEL and slice the onion as thinly as possible and fry in the oil for 10 minutes until soft and sweet.
SPLASH in the vinegar and sugar and heat for 5 minutes until the onions are sticky and marmalade-like.
ROLL out the pastry and cut out two rectangles about the size of your hand.
PLACE these on a greased or lined baking tray and score a 1cm margin around the edges.
PRICK the inner section of each rectangle all over with a fork and bake in the oven for 10 minutes until puffed up and golden.
CUT into that scored mark again and discard the top of the middle section. It should resemble a vol-au-vent with a lip around the edge and a well in the centre.
SPOON in some onion marmalade, crumble over goat's cheese and top with quartered cherry tomatoes and torn basil leaves.
RETURN to the oven for 5 minutes to melt the cheese and serve on a bed of dressed salad with halved olives.

NOTE!
Basil oil was once used as a perfume by Mediterranean prostitutes to attract customers. Perhaps not quite what you're looking for, but it is said to increase blood circulation, enhance sex drive and increase fertility!

MAIN
GORGONZOLA GNOCCHI WITH SPINACH AND TOASTED WALNUTS

2 large handfuls of fresh spinach
Potato gnocchi (250g)
Knob of butter
Double cream (50ml)
Handful of walnuts
Gorgonzola cheese (50g)
Parmesan

FILL a pan with salted water and bring to the boil.
WASH the spinach under cold running water and drain well.
DROP the gnocchi into the boiling water and cook for 4 minutes until they float.
WILT the spinach in a hot pan with the butter before adding the cream and walnuts.
CRUMBLE over the gorgonzola and season with freshly ground black pepper.
DRAIN the gnocchi and toss in the creamy spinach sauce.
DIVIDE between bowls and grate Parmesan over to serve.

DESSERT
BAILEYS SOUFFLÉ-STYLE
ICE CREAM

Whites of 2 large eggs (75ml)
Caster sugar (75g)
Double cream (150ml)
Handful of flaked almonds
Baileys to taste (40–50ml)
Fresh berries to serve

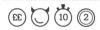

WHIP the egg whites until they hold in soft peaks, then gently fold in the caster sugar.

WHISK up the cream to the same stage in another bowl.

TOAST the almonds in a dry pan until golden.

FOLD the cream and egg whites together.

LACE with the Baileys and stir through the almonds so everything is well-combined.

SPOON into small teacups, ramekins or similar moulds.

COVER with cling film and freeze overnight.

DIP in hot water to loosen and turn out to serve.

GARNISH with fresh berries and more toasted almonds.

NOTE!
Technically this is not actually a soufflé, as it contains no egg yolk. But the light, airy consistency resembles one – they'll never know.

Maybe you owe your mates a favour, or you're thanking a neighbour for feeding the cat whilst you've been away topping up your tan, or just fancy a catch-up with friends surrounded by good food. This meal could be just the solution. The dangerously cheesy mushrooms, the garlicky twist on chicken Kiev and refreshing frozen torte to finish can all be pre-prepared, enabling you to chill out with your guests, knowing full well that every course will wow.

STARTER
STUFFED MUSHROOMS

4 large field mushrooms
Butter
Garlic-and-herb cream cheese
4 spring onions, finely sliced
Sprinkle of chilli flakes
8 rashers of bacon
2 ciabatta loaves, halved horizontally
Bowl of crisp salad leaves
Splash of salad dressing

sortedfood.com/
cheesestuffedmushrooms

PREHEAT the oven to 200°C.
BREAK off the stalks from the mushrooms and peel away any excess skin.
RUB the base of the mushrooms with butter, lay on a baking tray and season.
CREAM together the cheese, spring onions and chilli and spread into the cap of each mushroom.
BAKE for 10–15 minutes until softened.
GRILL the bacon until crispy and then pile it on top of the oozing cheese.
TOAST the bread under the grill.
SERVE the mushrooms on top of the bread, with a dressed side salad.

MAIN
DECONSTRUCTED CHICKEN KIEV

Chicken Kiev, originating from the capital of Ukraine, is a gorgeous dish that we've grown up with … although usually pre-prepared. But here we've deconstructed the classic chicken dish to make it easier without losing all of the best bits – succulent chicken, crispy breadcrumb and plenty of garlic butter.

For the chicken
3 cloves of garlic
Handful of fresh parsley
4 slices of white bread
Salted butter, melted (125g)
4 chicken breasts

To serve
12 cherry tomatoes
12 black olives
Small chunk of feta cheese
Drizzle of olive oil
Boiled new potatoes

sortedfood.com/
chickenkiev

PREHEAT the oven to 220°C.
PEEL and chop the garlic.
WASH and chop the parsley.
STICK the bread into a food processor and blitz until you have crumbs.
POUR the butter, garlic, parsley and some salt and pepper into the processor and blitz for another second.
TRIM any sinew or fat from the chicken and score the top of the breasts.
TIP the garlic breadcrumbs onto a baking tray, pat into a layer ½cm thick and place onto each breast.
BAKE the chicken for 20 minutes to cook through and so the herb crust goes golden brown and crispy.
HALVE the cherry tomatoes and olives and crumble the feta.
MIX together, with a drizzle of oil and salt and pepper for the simplest and tastiest salad.
SERVE with the new potatoes as a light summer meal.

DESSERT
ICED LEMON AND GINGER TORTES

Make this whenever you're bored and have time. They'll keep in the freezer (if wrapped in cling film) for well over a month, and will always be on hand when you need a cracking pudding at a moment's notice. The perfect end to any dinner date!

Ginger nut biscuits (200g)
Melted butter (70g)
2 large eggs
Double cream (130ml)
Caster sugar (60g)
Zest and juice of 2 lemons
Fresh berries to serve

BASH up the biscuits in a plastic bag with a hefty rolling pin.
MELT the butter over a gentle heat or in the microwave and combine with the biscuit crumbs.
PRESS the mixture down firmly into four dessert rings on a tray and chill.
SEPARATE the whites and the yolks of the eggs into two clean bowls.
WHISK the egg white to stiff peaks.
WHIP the cream to soft peaks in another bowl.
BEAT the sugar into the egg yolk and add the lemon zest and juice.
FOLD in the egg white, then the cream, and pour onto the prepared biscuit bases.
FREEZE for at least 4 hours.
WARM the edges of the rings slightly with the palms of your hands to ease out the tortes.
SERVE with a few fresh berries.

TIP
If you don't have individual dessert rings then just save small tins (e.g. beans or tuna), wash thoroughly and open both ends – just be careful of any sharp edges.

INDEX

311

THANKS

JUST LIKE ANY GOOD RECIPE,
SORTED HAS TAKEN A MIXTURE
OF THE RIGHT INGREDIENTS
TO GET HERE AND MAKE
SURE WE DIDN'T END UP AS A
SUNKEN SOUFFLÉ. THEY SAY
THAT TOO MANY COOKS SPOIL
THE BROTH, BUT THE TRUTH
IS WE WOULDN'T BE HERE
WITHOUT THE HELP OF A LOT
OF OTHER PEOPLE.

WHETHER THEY ARE FRIENDS
FROM SCHOOL, UNIVERSITY,
YOUTUBE, OR 'THE INDUSTRY',
EACH PERSON HAS PLAYED
THEIR PART IN CREATING BOTH
THIS BOOK AND THE ENTIRE
SORTED WORLD ...

FOR THESE PEOPLE AND YOU
GUYS AT HOME, THE NEXT
ROUND IS ON US!

ADAM WILKINSON
ALEX DAY
ALEX PAGE
ALFIE DEYES
BARRY TAYLOR
BEN EBBRELL
BETH FOX-FULLER
BORRA GARSON
BUBZBEAUTY
CHARLIE MCDONNELL
CHIS KENDALL
CHRIS BINGHAM
CHRIS BRYANT-
MANSELL
CHRIS FERGUSSON
DAMIEN MARCHI
DAVE DAYS
DESTORM
EMILY BRENNAN
FLEUR DE FORCE
FRANCES COTTRELL
GABRIELLE WILSON
GARY HIGGINS
GORDON DAY
HAYLEY JONES
INGRID
JACK KENNERLEY
JAMES SILVERSTONE
JAMIE SPAFFORD
JENNA MARBLES
JESS LIZAMA
JOE PENNA
JON GAVAGHAN
JON ROSER
JOSH REID

JOSH TAYLOR
JUSTINE EZARIK
LAUREN SHOEBOTTOM
LINDSEY EVANS
LORA GRANT
LUCY WILSON
MARCUS BUTLER
MARTIN STIRLING
MATTHEW WAITE
MIKE HUTTLESTONE
NICOLA KNIGHT
OLGA KAY
PENNY JONES
RACHAEL PIKE
RAY TAYLOR
RICHARD SMITH
ROB MADIN
SABINA SMITHAM
SAM NORTON
SARAH PENNA
STE ANDERSON
STEVE CAMPBELL
STEVE LAU
TOM BARNES
TOM HEMSLEY
TOM MOODY
TOM RIDGEWELL
TORYN WESTCOTT